The New Complete
Yorkshire Terrier

There are many versions of beauty in the world of purebred dogs, but nothing quite matches the look of a fine Yorkshire Terrier in top condition. The model here, Ch. Shadomountin Steppin' Up mirrors this well. Owned by Janet Jackson and bred by Edward and Kathy Bucher, he is shown just after winning the Yorkshire Terrier Club of America Specialty in 1985 under judge Michael J. Suave. *DiGiacomo*

The New Complete
Yorkshire Terrier

Joan B. Gordon

**HOWELL
BOOK HOUSE**

New York

Howell Book House
Macmillan General Reference
A Simon & Schuster Macmillan Company
1633 Broadway
New York, NY 10019-6785

Library of Congress Cataloging-in-Publication Data

Gordon, Joan B.
    The new complete Yorkshire terrier / Joan B. Gordon.
        p.   cm.
    Rev. ed. of: The complete Yorkshire terrier. 1st. ed. 1976.
    ISBN 0-87605-361-4
    1. Yorkshire terriers.   I. Gordon, Joan B.   Complete Yorkshire
    terrier.   II. Title.
    SF429.Y6G63   1993
    636.7'6—dc20   92-41046
                                                             CIP

10   9   8   7   6   5

Printed in the United States of America

To

the memory of my sister Janet E. Bennett.
Wildweir would never have existed without her help,
encouragement, knowledge and above all her
companionship . . .

. . . and to my husband, Stu, without whose
help and encouragement I could not have continued
to breed and show Yorkshire Terriers.

"Mirror, mirror on a stand, who is the fairest in the land?" Ch. Dot's Top Banana, bred and owned by Dorothy Gaunt. *Missy Yuhl*

Contents

OUT HUNTING

Jeanne Grimsley

Appreciations

I would like to express my sincere thanks to Shirley Patterson who took on the job of writing the obedience section, a subject I admit to having very little knowledge of.

Also to Shirley Patterson for the adult head study; Jeanne Grimsby for the lovely original illustrations that grace this book; and Elissa Taddie for her fine sketches and charts of the Yorkie coat pattern.

And to all the Wildweir Yorkies who have supervised my work especially "Sam," Ch. Wildweir Star Sampler who assisted, if it can be called that, with the typing.

Joan B. Gordon (*right*), author of *The New Complete Yorkshire Terrier*, showing with her sister, the late Janet E. Bennett. Although this edition is the work of Mrs. Gordon, it reflects the collaboration of both sisters that resulted in the first edition. They are shown here with Ch. Wildweir Doorprize (*left*) and Ch. Wildweir Catchphrase, homebred litter sisters.

The Author

IN THE CONTEMPORARY FANCY of the purebred dog, it is all too commonplace to find an individual described as an "institution" whether that person merits that description or not. Joan B. Gordon earns that description for her own activity in dogs and what she has been a part of for such a long time—Wildweir.

Wildweir, the prefix she and her late twin sister Janet E. Bennett established in 1950, has a peerless record of achievements and has positively impacted the Yorkshire Terrier for all time. This applies both to the conformation ring and to the Yorkshire's total gene pool.

Wildweir has bred or owned some 240 champions; over 155 of these have been homebreds. The foundation stock for the Wildweir Yorkshires was drawn from the finest families in the breed at the time. That the insightful blending worked is proven by the kennel's producing record and by the fact that Wildweir Yorkshires form the basis for so many successful families that came later. From Wildweir came the all-time top-producing sire in the history of the breed. When one considers the normally small size of Yorkshire litters, the ninety-five champion get of Ch. Wildweir Pomp N' Circumstance qualifies as a towering achievement for a breeder.

Joan Gordon and Janet Bennett have piloted their dogs to numerous Best in Show and Group victories as well as many top Specialty awards from one coast of America to the other—*and they did it themselves!* Westminster, International and Harbor Cities are just three of the most distinguished events at which Wildweirs made history.

When the current Yorkshire Terrier Club of America was formed in 1951, the sisters became charter members and in the ensuing years gave freely of their time and talent to make and keep the Club a smoothly functioning organization. In more ways than many realize, the Yorkshire Terrier has benefitted greatly from the interest and involvement of Joan Gordon and Janet Bennett.

That they should have been the source of *The Complete Yorkshire Terrier*, the original edition of this book, is consistent with another activity they conducted for the sake of their chosen breed. Today, Joan Gordon presides over the results of decades of research compiling the record of every champion, every important win and every significant event in the history of the Yorkshire Terrier. Her priceless collection of books, photos, illustrations and miscellany on this glorious Toy treasure is probably unexcelled throughout the world.

When *The Complete Yorkshire Terrier* first appeared in 1976, fanciers had at their disposal the finest reference ever published on the breed. Now, the first new edition of this landmark work, *The New Complete Yorkshire Terrier* updates the breed's story and furnishes a splendid bounty of guidance and breed knowledge for every friend of the Yorkshire Terrier today.

Preface to
the First Edition

I N 1891, Mr. P. H. Coombs in *The American Book of the Dog* wisely cautioned: "It is quite an undertaking to breed a Yorkshire combining the proper colors, texture of coat and Terrier type; and no amount of care or attention on the part of the owner can turn a badly-bred, ill-formed specimen into a good one."

Coat texture and hair colors are inherited. Bred in, the wrong coat texture can be counted on to arrive on a well-composed Yorkie as readily as on an ill-composed one. Similarly, wrong hair colors bred in find their way on to well-formed and ill-formed specimens alike.

Well-bred Yorkies are obtainable; breeders with knowledge and experience offer Yorkies that will grow into adults that are as sound as possible in all features. But it is important that the well-bred Yorkie be wisely bred in turn, and spared such indiscriminate matings as suffered by the dog of which Philipp Gruening wrote in *The Dobermann Pinscher* "They took this great mansion and tore it down to build hovels."

Thankfully, all across the country there are breeders who are holding the line and producing Yorkies that meet the standard—lovely gold and blue dogs. Sound dogs, too, of fine health and disposition, with well-proportioned bodies that enable them to show, to enjoy their owner's lives and to produce in top-flight style. And because they model the AKC-approved standard, they are correct in type.

If this book helps new judges, new exhibitors, and particularly new breeders, to recognize them and to seek them out, it will have served our aim.

JOAN B. GORDON

JANET E. BENNETT

The New Complete
Yorkshire Terrier

This interesting study of British prize winners circa 1878 shows that even then the Yorkshire Terrier's (#6) diminutive size was already established.

1

Manufacture of the Yorkshire Terrier

THOUGH many breed histories would make it appear so, the Yorkshire Terrier is not a breed drawn from thin air.

Too many of these histories are, alas, no more than folklore gleaned from pages of other books, whose authors did little research. Contrary to their claims, the origins, early history and cultivation of the Yorkshire terrier are not lost in the mists of time. Nor do they lie buried in the cunning, crafty minds of the Yorkshire weavers. The warp and woof of how this silken terrier came into the world of purebred dogs *can* be traced.

Included in the theories offered regarding the production of the Yorkshire Terrier are that it was bred from a large dog like an Airedale, from a smooth-coated dog like a Manchester, or from a short-legged, long-backed, uneven toplined dog such as a Dandie Dinmont. The reasoning given for these breeds is that they are born black and tan, and some change color to blue and tan. But if that be the basis, why not say the Doberman Pinscher, or even add a dash of the Chow?

These authorities then throw in the Maltese, to explain how the Yorkshire acquired a silky coat. In this, their reasoning is more understandable, but hardly solid. For the Maltese and Yorkshire merger, if it did happen, came into the picture after the Yorkshire had already taken its place in The Kennel Club Stud Book.

That there are certain genetic factors that these breeds hold in common with the Yorkshire Terrier is undeniable. But easy as it might be to do so, this is no cause to make them the genetic ancestors of the Yorkie. For all dogs originally came from the same stock, and so carry the same factors to an extent, depending upon what was sought to form the required animal.

Color in dogs, for example, is formed by various genes. The two basic colors are yellow and dark brown (or black). They are controlled by other genes to allow the color pattern, color distribution and the depth or dilution of the color. The hair texture is controlled by another set of genes. The size of the dog is controlled by other genes, as are head shape, ear shape, tail carriage and so on.

With this in mind, how could the Yorkshire have been developed in a few short years? The answer lies in a study of the history of the dogs of its birthland, Great Britain, with a search for a dog that had the basic factors required by the first Yorkshire Terrier breeders.

TRACING THE FACTORS

The Waterside Terrier

In the early years of dogs in Great Britain almost all hunting land was denied to the serfs. To keep them from poaching with hunting dogs, laws were written that date as far back as the Canons of Canute in the eleventh century. However, the serfs were allowed ''the little dogs'' because ''it stands to reason that there is no danger in them.''

These insignificant little Toy dogs were not of any Spaniel breed, for Spaniels could not be kept in a forest without a special grant. The determinant as to whether or not a serf might keep a dog was size. The foresters were provided with a fixed gauge, a hoop, and only the little dogs that could pass through the seven-inch diameter of the hoop could be owned by the serfs.

These little dogs went into the fields with the mowers to kill the rats. They killed the rabbits in the vegetable patch, and in general kept the poor man's home safe from rats and other varmints, as well as supplying small game from the fields and hedgerows for his table.

By the time of William IV (1765–1835) the Waterside Terrier, a small, longish-coated dog, occasionally grizzly (bluish-gray) in color, was common in Yorkshire. In an article in *The English Stockkeeper* (1887), G. H. Wilkinson reported:

I have been at some trouble looking up several old fanciers, one of whom is Mr. John Richardson of Halifax who is now in his 67th year, and very interesting it was to hear this aged man go back to "the good old days" of over half a century ago. Fifty years ago, there was in Halifax, and the immediate neighborhood, a type of dog called at that time (and even within these last twenty years) a "Waterside Terrier," a game little dog, varying in weight from six to twenty pounds, mostly about ten pounds weight—a dog resembling the present Welsh and Airedale Terrier on a small scale. At this period, these dogs were bred for the purpose of hunting and killing rats. They would go into the river with a ferret, and were just in their element when put into a rat pit. An almost daily occurrence at that time was to back them to kill a given number of rats in a given time.

It seems a pity that such a breed should have become extinct. Mr. Richardson himself owned a little bitch "Polly," who weighed six pounds and she was frequently put into a rat pit with a dozen rats, the whole of which she would speedily kill against time. She would also swim the river and hunt with the ferret. This little bitch, I am told, had four or five inches of coat on each side of her body, with a white or silver head.

These little Waterside Terriers, with their ratting ability, more than likely traveled all the rivers, backwaters and canals along which early commerce, from the Shires to Scotland, moved prior to railroads and roadways.

In fact, the little Terrier journeyed down around the Horn to the vast Australian continent. Along with its ratting abilities, this small Terrier's faculties as a watchdog made it invaluable to the free settlers of the frontier lands of the vast Crown Colonies in the Southern Pacific. *The Australian Terrier and the Australian Silky Terrier,* by W. A. Wheatland, contains the following:

In discussing the breed with Mr. Scott, of Ross, Tasmania, whose family have resided in the district for over a hundred years, he stated:

"It is known that sometime prior to 1820, the free settlers of the Midlands of Tasmania in the areas of Campbelltown and Ross successfully bred Broken-Coated Terrier Dogs of a blue-sheen body colour,

The Otter Terrier, steel engraving, circa 1858 by W. P. Smith.

The terrier tribe of the early nineteenth century was a mixed lot to say the least. This famous engraving by Sydenham Edwards, "The Terrier," appeared in his *Cynographia Britannica,* circa 1800, and gives some idea of the variety of type in the early "earth dogs." It is from this eclectic gene pool that the modern Yorkshire Terrier ultimately evolved.

"Ratcatchers" from a painting, possibly by Sir Edwin Landseer, circa 1821. The models were the Scotch Terriers, "Vixen," "Brutus" and "Boxer."

with tan legs and face and weighing approximately seven to ten pounds. In those days, marauding Aboriginals, bushrangers, and escaped convicts were prevalent in these districts. It was the unerring and uncanny instinct of these Blue and Tan Terriers to detect the approach of strangers at great distances that made them a prized possession as watchdogs and safeguards around the home. They were extremely hard to come by, the individual strains being most jealously guarded.''

By 1872, Mr. J. Spink, one of the original Yorkshire Terrier breeders, had exported Punch, a grandson of Old Sandy out of a Halifax bitch, to Norman D'Arcy, Brisbane, Queensland, Australia. Old Sandy was also the grandsire of Huddersfield Ben, the first dog to receive the designation of Yorkshire Terrier. Punch is listed as having won prizes at thirteen shows in England prior to his exportation to Australia.

Here, in the Waterside Terrier, lay a supply of genes for silky coats, small size, and blue and tan pattern. It is in this ancient breed, too, that we find the reason that the Airedale has been mistakenly theorized to be an ancestor of the Yorkie.

Children play a game at parties where one whispers something into another's ears, and it is repeated from ear to ear until the last child tells the version he's heard, which is always strangely removed from the original. An old breeder of Yorkies may well have said, ''Well, we used the Waterside Terrier in their origin,'' and that statement may have been repeated down the line. Some years later—in about the late 1890s—a writer, searching for the breed's origin, hears that it was made from a Waterside Terrier, and immediately conceives it to be descended from the Airedale. For when the Yorkshire men living in the dale of the river Aire had wanted a dog with the virtues of the Waterside Terrier, but larger—a dog with the ability to hunt larger game along the riverbank and in the water—they found their answer in combining their Terrier with the Otter Hound. The resulting dog was, at first, still called a Waterside Terrier and classes were provided at early dog shows. At last, at Birmingham in 1883, the classes were for Waterside *or* Airedale Terriers. Soon it officially became the Airedale Terrier and the little Waterside Terrier, as such, vanished from the scene. Thus, the writer of the late 1890s, knowing that in its early days the Airedale Terrier had been called a Waterside Terrier, puts his facts back to front, and identifies the Airedale as the Yorkie's unknown factor.

The Clydesdale and the Paisley Terriers

With the beginnings of the Industrial Revolution in the later years of the 1700s, the displaced crofters of Scotland, their clans broken, went south to Yorkshire, England's largest shire. In fact, Yorkshire was so large that, in the days of horse transport, it was divided into Ridings—East, North and West—each an area that could be covered on a horse in a given time. The West Riding included the large industrial towns of Halifax and Bradford. Nearby, across the county border in Lancashire, was the manufacturing city of Manchester. There, these displaced men and women found work as weavers and brought with them their little dogs, unwittingly adding confusion to the facts of the Yorkshire's origin.

Rawdon B. Lee, speaking of Yorkshire Terriers in *Modern Dogs (Terriers)* says: "How the name of Scotch Terrier became attached to a dog which so thoroughly had its home in Yorkshire and Lancashire is somewhat difficult to determine, if it can be determined at all, but a very old breeder of the variety told me that the first of them came from Scotland, where they had been accidently produced from a cross between the silk-coated Skye (the Clydesdale) and the black and tan Terrier. One could scarcely expect that a pretty dog, partaking in a degree after both its parents, could be produced from a smooth-coated dog, a long-coated bitch or vice versa. Maybe, two or three animals so bred had been brought by some of the Paisley weavers into Yorkshire and there, suitably admired, pains were taken to perpetuate the strain." Though Mr. Lee helps here to add confusion, at least it's nice to see one early skeptic of a smooth-coated breed being a factor.

Scotland with its mountain highlands limited the communication between the dwellers in their highland fastness and their lowland counterparts. The isolation and the segregation of the Scottish clans and Scottish people gave each room to develop a dog to fit his requirements: the Scotchman of the Isles bred one type, the Highlander another, and the man of the heath and moor developed yet another.

These Terriers acquired their names from their work, their area of origin, or the estates of individual owners. Names included Aberdeen, Highland, Cairn, Skye, Short-coated Skye, Lowland, Roseneath, Paisley, Clydesdale, Diehard, Otter Terrier, Sorty Terrier and so on. But *all* were also catalogued as Scotch Terriers.

In 1822, *The History of Quadrupeds* describes the Scotch Terrier as "rough; short-legged; long-backed; very strong and most commonly of a yellow color mixed with black and white."

It would have been a considerable help in unraveling canine history if breed names had been standardized when language was first invented. If dog shows have done nothing else for the different breeds, they have at least given them distinctive names and standards which belong to no other breed. Certainly the early Scotch Terriers could have benefited by an earlier sorting.

These Terriers, coming into England from Scotland, were referred to in the 1800s as Scotch Terriers. The Aberdeen Terrier finally grabbed the title closest to this nomenclature by becoming the Scottish Terrier. The first Scottish Terrier standard called for a weight between fifteen to twenty pounds. The first volume of the Scottish Terrier Club of Scotland, published in 1895, almost ten years after the breed's finding a place in the Kennel Club Stud Book, registers the dogs under the following colors: black-brown on legs; black face and legs brown; dark, steel gray; steel gray, white on chest; red-gray brindle; black, brown of face and legs; plus the usual colors.

The Scotch Terrier that has the most interesting factors for the Yorkshire Terrier is the early Skye Terrier. From *Terriers, Their Points and Management* (F. T. Barton, 1918), we get: "What are sometimes described as Roseneath (Roseneath being in the Island of Bute) Terriers appear to have been the original type of Skye. These Terriers are described as of a fawn or silver gray and from 10 to 16 lbs." Also, in describing the early Skye, the same author says: "The small size of these Terriers and their handsome appearance has had a great deal to do with these little dogs being so much sought after." Their weight is given as dogs sixteen to twenty pounds; bitches, sixteen pounds; height at shoulders, nine inches for dogs, eight and a half inches for bitches; length from the back of the head to tail set-on, twenty two and a half inches. The coat was not to be silky.

The fanciers of the Skye had a problem in settling the breed to type. The early Skyes, before standards were set, produced what was called a soft-coated, prick-eared Skye. Sometimes it was called a Linty or a Glasgow Silky. Out of this confusion came the Skye Terrier—a dog with a long, hard, flat coat and an undercoat—and two breeds that have been swept from sight, the Clydesdale Terrier and the Paisley Terrier.

Much confusion remains today in articles written about the

Scotch Terrier. Detail from a painting by Sir Joshua Reynolds, 1776.

The Clydesdale Terrier, Balloch Myle Wee Wattie, circa 1904. Compare this drop-eared specimen with the dog in the illustration below.

Hazy of Johnstounburn, a Scottish-bred Yorkshire, circa 1950, owned by Mrs. Crookshank, was the dam of champions. There are probably more similarities than differences between Hazy and the Clydesdale.

Clydesdale and Paisley. Most authors conceive them to be one and the same breed, which they probably were until fanciers started selecting and breeding them to a fixed standard. In *The Dogs of Scotland* (1891), the author, D. J. Thompson Grey, gives the following on the Paisley or Clydesdale Terrier:

> Blackhall writing in the *Scottish Terrier* for June, 1884 says: "It will be in the recollection of many readers that nine or ten years ago this Terrier exercised breeders of the Skye Terrier considerably, and week after week was the occasion of, shall I say, interesting? friendly? or interested? correspondence in *The Country and Fancier's Chronicle* or *Livestock Journal,* when behind the unsicklier shelter of nom de plumes, our Skye Terrier friends wrote up their own dogs and decried those of the opposition.
>
> "This paper warfare was continued with increasing acrimony, fresh combatants being enlisted on the various sides, until in the interest of general readers, who were doubtless beginning to grumble at the flat, stale, and unprofitable character of their threepence worth, the editors added their quota to the subject—viz: This correspondence must now cease. *Ed.*
>
> "There being no separate classes for fancy Terriers, they were exhibited in the Skye Terrier classes and very frequently carried off the honors. However, the aforesaid correspondence served at least one good purpose in deciding once and for all, that the Skye Terrier must have a hard coat, thus ousting one of the 'Dromios' from a false position.
>
> "That decision was well-nigh the death of the silky-haired Terrier, as at no show, even under the new arrangement, with exception of one or two in the west country, were the boycotted Terriers provided for. The only opening left being the unsatisfactory 'any other variety class.' It is therefore, no cause for wonder that, under these adverse circumstances, interest in the breed rapidly waned, and but for the effort made by a very few admirers to keep them on their legs, this popular dog would soon have degenerated into a mongrel and have been deposited upon the silent shore of memory."

The Clydesdale Terrier did not get washed ashore but kept afloat as late as the 1900s, having a place in The Kennel Club and the AKC Stud Books. The Paisley stayed afloat long enough to have a standard drawn up in 1884. These two Terriers probably were the result of breeding soft-coated, prick-eared Skyes and were both developed in the vale of the Clyde river, one of whose river markets is Paisley. Their breed standards and descriptions show them to have had somewhat different requirements, though the wording of their standards should have given a clue as to where they ultimately came to rest.

Mr. Freeman Lloyd in the AKC publication, *Pure-Bred Dogs–American Kennel Gazette*, March 31, 1934, described the Paisley Terrier in an article on "Many Dogs in Many Lands":

One of the handsomest of Scottish breeds was the Clydesdale or Paisley Terrier, which has unfortunately died out. At least, I have not seen one for years. This dog was sometimes known as the Glasgow Terrier. It came into prominence in the middle '80s of the last century. Of all the "fancy dogs," this creature, in full coat, was easily the most delightful. Imagine a dog of the same build in body and head as a first-class, 18 lb. Skye Terrier. Visualize it with the same prick-ears. Think of such a dog covered with long hair often trailing on the ground; the hair being of the same color and fibre as the silk or spun-glass-like quality, of that carried by a real exquisite specimen of the Yorkshire Terrier at its very best. That was the Paisley Terrier from the Dale of the Clyde.

The author says further on:

Were it possible to bench a row of representative dogs of this kind at a Westminster Show, the animal would attract great attention, even among the luxurious class that visit Madison Square Garden. To give a word picture of the breed is difficult. One of the most attractive points was the heavily-fringed, upright ears. The silky hair hung like the mantilla of a Spanish senorita. The body and headcoat were perfectly flat and free from any trace of curl or waviness; very glossy and silky in texture (not linty) and without any pily undercoat as is found in the Skye Terrier.

The colors ranged from dark blue to light fawn. The most desired were the various shades of blue. Dark blue was preferred, but without any approach to blackness. The color of the head was best liked when of a beautiful silvery blue, which became darker on the ears. The back, or body coat varied in its shades of blue, inclining to silvery on the lowest parts of the body and legs. The tail was generally of the same shade, or a little darker than the back.

Some day, perhaps, we shall again see the Clydesdale, Paisley, or Glasgow Terrier. If he be but a soft-coated Skye Terrier, he will be like some attractive exotic amid the sterner dogs of the land of Burns and of Scott, both dog lovers to the core.

The Paisley Terrier standard drawn up in 1884 called for color to be "various shades of blue, dark blue for preference. The hair on head and lower extremities slightly lighter than the body color, but it should not approach a linty shade." [Lint in this case signified flax, therefore a light straw color].

Unfortunately, the Paisley Terrier fanciers threw in their lot with the Skye Terrier club and disappeared from view. A few Glasgow fanciers formed themselves into a club and resolved to change their breed name from Paisley to Clydesdale Terrier. It would seem that the Glasgow fanciers had dogs that carried strong factors for that "linty" shade.

Captain W. Wilmer in *The Book of the Dog*, writes: "The Clydesdale may be described as an anomaly. He stands as it were upon a pedestal of his own; and unlike other Scotch Terriers he is classified as Non-Sporting. Perhaps his marvelously fine and silky coat precludes him from the rough work of hunting vermin, though it is certain his gamelike instincts would naturally lead him to do so. Of all Scotch dogs he is perhaps the smallest; his weight seldom exceeding 18 lbs."

The breed standard described him as:

A long, low, level dog, with heavily fringed erect ears and a long coat like the finest silk or spun glass, which hangs quite straight and evenly down each side, from a parting extending from the nose to the root of the tail. *Color*: A level, bright steel blue extending from the back of the head to the root of tail, and on no account intermingled with any fawn, light or dark hairs. The head, legs and feet should be a clear bright golden tan, free from grey, sooty or dark hairs. The tail should be very dark blue or black. *Coat*: as long and straight as possible, free from all trace of curl or waviness, very glossy and silky in texture with an entire absence of undercoat.

Thus the blue and silver Paisley had become a blue and golden tan Clydesdale who found a place in The Kennel Club Stud Book and, for a few years, in the American Kennel Club Stud Book.

From the North Sea, the Scottish border marches westward with the border of the shire of York, forming the northern boundary line of England. The Yorkshire border turns southward to end and turns east at the Cathedral City of York. To the west, in the shire of Lancaster, is the large manufacturing city of Manchester and this area holds another factor that was needed to produce the Yorkshire Terrier.

The old English working Terriers of the Manchester area were first described in 1771 in a book called *The History of Manchester*, by Whitaker. The dogs of that area are described as "Little Terrars of black and tan and sometimes white and red, with crooked legs and shaggy hair."

From these shaggy haired dogs was developed the smooth silky coated old black and tan Terrier or Manchester Terrier. At a show in

A Clydesdale Terrier from the turn of the century showing erect ears. This now extinct breed occurred with drop or erect ears.

The Paisley Terrier, Mr. John King's Lorne of Paisely.

Holburn in 1862, there were forty-two benched, divided equally in two classes, one for animals over five pounds, the other for dogs and bitches under five pounds.

In *The Dog in Health and Disease*, "Stonehenge" (nom-de-plume of J. H. Walsh) describes the black and tan Terrier's color as "The only true color is black and tan . . . but many puppies are marked with white, even so much as to predominate in white and sometimes, but rarely, they are blue." Mr. Rawdon Lee says, "Before closing the chapter (black and tan Terriers), allusion must be made to the 'blue' or slate-colored Terriers which are occasionally obtained from this variety, though the parents may be correctly marked themselves. Such 'sports' are in reality as well bred as the real article and are found in all sizes, perhaps most commonly amongst the 'toys' and the small-sized specimens, than amongst the larger ones. Some are entirely 'blue' or slate-colored, others have tan markings."

There were many other English Terriers in the Yorkshire and Lancashire area that were rough-coated and of a black and tan pattern. They were small enough to be carried in a hunter's pouch. But without popular support they have passed from the scene or have been lost in some recognized Terrier breed. Like the Terriers from Scotland, the old English Terriers were named for their ability, color or place of origin. Though there were many Terriers from Manchester, the black and tan smooth-coated became so indentified with Manchester that he became officially the Manchester Terrier. There were also in the area, dogs that were black and tan with white markings, grizzle and tan, rough, wire-haired, broken-haired and silky-coated. Plenty of factors to choose from.

All of the aforementioned dogs obviously carried the genes to produce coat patterns of black and tan, and the genes to dilute the black to blue or grizzle. Dogs, in some strains, carried the factor to clear the black to golden tan at maturity. Some of these breeds carry the factors to produce a glossy silk coat, in some short and others long. Here then, in these Scotch and old English Terriers lay the greatest genetic bank to produce the Yorkshire as we now know him; a combination of the dog the Scottish weavers took south to the large industrial towns where, with the Yorkshiremen, they interwove the strands of the local dogs of Manchester, Halifax, Bradford and Leeds.

All that was needed at this point were fanciers ready to breed the Yorkie's points and to show its merit in the rapidly developing show rings. Through them, it would soon advance to the fore, burying the Waterside, Paisley and Clydesdale Terrier in its silken wake.

THE WEAVING OF THE BREED

It has been hard for many writers to accept the almost overnight production of the Yorkshire Terrier—a dog that within a few years of its introduction was producing dogs under five pounds, with clear golden tan and blue silky coats, reaching to twelve inches in length. *The American Book of the Dog,* written in 1891 by P. H. Coombs, provides some answers. Mr. Coombs, an American pioneer of the breed, had gathered the story from the last of the generation who knew the Yorkie's beginnings. In his chapter on the Yorkshire terrier in the book, he wrote:

> No doubt much difficulty has been experienced in obtaining information relating to its early history; and one opinion expressed by Shaw, seems to be that substantially the history was known, but that it was kept a secret. It would be manifestly unjust to deprive the Yorkshire Terrier of the title to a pedigree running back to the progenitors of the breed.
>
> In an interesting article of this breed, published in the *Century Magazine* in 1886 and written by Mr. James Watson of Philadelphia, is given about the first public information tending to positively identify its origin—to a certain extent at least. The writer says: "Some of our authorities have attempted to throw a great deal of mystery about the origin of the Yorkshire terrier, where none really exists. If we consider that the mill operatives (*workers*), who originated the breed by careful selection of the best long-coated small Terriers they could find, were all ignorant men, unaccustomed to imparting information for public use, we may see some reason why reliable facts have not been easily attained. These early writers show but little knowledge of the possibilities of selection. Stonehenge, for instance, in his early editions, speaks of it being impossible for a dog with a three-inch coat and seven-inch beard to be a descendant of the soft-coated Scotch Terrier, without a cross of some kind. The absurdity of this is seen when we remember that within a few years of the date of his history, Yorkshire Terriers were shown with twelve inches of coat. Then, again, he speaks of the King Charles Spaniel as being employed to give the blue and tan, a more ridiculous statement than which could not have been penned. To get a blue and tan, long, straight, silky coat, breeders were not likely to employ a

Mr. Spink's "Bounce" a grandson of Kitty and Old Crab, resolutely maintains possession of the trophy coveted by the other old-time terriers depicted in this woodcut from *Dogs of the British Isles*, 1872. The excerpt below is from the same book.

THE YORKSHIRE BLUE-TAN SILKY COATED TERRIER.

THE last dog in the frontispiece is Mr. Spink's Bounce, a good specimen of the modern silky-haired blue-tan terrier, but not quite coming up to some of those which have been exhibited since 1865, whose coat is considerably longer, and, if possible, more silky. Excepting in colour and coat, this dog resembles the old English rough terrier, the shapes of body and head being exactly the same.

The ears are generally cropped, but if entire should be fine, thin, and moderately small. The coat should be long, very silky in texture, and completely parted down the back—the beard being often two or three inches in length, and entirely of a golden tan colour. The colour must be entirely blue on the back and down to the elbow and thigh, showing a rich lustre, and without any admixture of tan. The legs and muzzle should be a rich golden tan. Ears also tan, but darker in shade; the colour on the top of the skull becomes lighter, approaching to fawn, the two shades gradually merging into each other. Weight, 10lb. to 18lb.

Value of Points of the Yorkshire Blue-tan.

Colour—		Coat—		Ears 10	Symmetry—	
Good blue, without tan 25		Length 15			Like that of	
Good tan 25		Silkyness ... 10			Scotch terrier 15	
	50		25	10		15

Grand total, **100.**

The silver-grey Yorkshire terrier is not a distinct breed, being merely a paler variety of the blue-tan.

black and tan dog with a wide chest, tuck-up loin, a round bullet head, large protruding eyes, and heavy Spaniel ears. The idea is too absurd to be entertained for a moment. As arrayed against all the conjectures of theorists, I have in my possession a letter from Mrs. M. A. Foster, of Bradford, England who, in writing of the dog Bradford Hero, the winner of ninety-seven first prizes, says; "The pedigree of Bradford Hero includes all the best dogs for thirty-five years back, and they were all Scotch Terriers, the name Yorkshire given them on account of their being improved so much in that region."

Following this, and about a year later, Mr. Ed. Bootman of Halifax, England furnished an article on the origin of the breed, for publication in the *English Stockkeeper*, which that journal, "feeling the importance of all facts relating to the origin of the breed," published as follows:

"Swift's Old Crab, a cross-bred Scotch Terrier, Kershaw's Kitty, a Skye, and an Old English Terrier bitch kept by J. Whittam, then residing in Hatter's Fold, Halifax, were the progenitors of the present race of Yorkshire Terriers. These dogs were in the zenith of their fame forty years ago. The owner of Old Crab was a native of Halifax, and a joiner by trade [*joiner—a carpenter*]. He worked at Oldham for some time as a journeyman [*hired by the day*], and then removed to Manchester, where he kept a public house. Whether he got Crab at Oldham or Manchester I have not been able to ascertain. He had him when in Manchester, and from there sent him several times to Halifax on a visit to Kitty. The last would be about 1850.

"Crab was a dog of about eight or nine lbs. weight, with a good Terrier head and eye, but with a long body, resembling the Scotch Terrier. The legs and muzzle only were tanned, and the hair on the body would be about three or four inches in length. He has stood for years in a case in a room at the Westgate Hotel, a public house which his owner kept when he returned to his native town, where, I believe, the dog may be seen today.

"Kitty was a bitch different in type from Crab. She was a drop-eared Skye, with plenty of coat of a blue shade, but destitute of tan on any part of the body. Like Crab, she had no pedigree. She was originally stolen from Manchester and sent to a man named Jackson, a saddler in Huddersfield, who, when it became known that a five pound reward was offered in Manchester for her recovery, sent her to a person named Harrison, then a waiter at the White Swan Hotel, Halifax, to escape detection, and from Harrison she passed into the hand of Mr. J. Kershaw of Beshop Blaise, a public house which once stood on the Old North Bridge, Halifax. Prior to 1851 Kitty had six litters, all of which were by Crab. In these six litters she had thirty-six puppies, twenty-eight of which were dogs, and served to stock the district with rising sires. After

1851, when she passed into the possession of Mr. F. Jagger, she had forty-four puppies, making a total of eighty.

"Mr. Whittam's bitch, whose name I cannot get to know, was an Old English Terrier, with tanned head, ears and legs, and a sort of grizzle back. She was built on the lines of speed. Like the others, she had no pedigree. She was sent to the late Bernard Hartley of Allen Gate, Halifax by a friend residing in Scotland. When Mr. Hartley had got tired of her, he gave her to his coachman, Mason, who, in turn, gave her to his friend Whittam, and Whittam used her years for breeding purposes. Although this bitch came from Scotland, it is believed the parents were from this district."

The last-named writer has so fully identified the three dogs first employed to manufacture the breed, together with their names, ownership, characteristics, and other facts concerning them, that there can be no doubt as to the authenticity of the history of the origin of the breed. His history, published in *The Stockkeeper* in 1887, has never been publicly contradicted, and it is evident that there can now be no grounds for following the reasoning of writers who claim that the origin is a mystery.

We agree whole-heartedly with Mr. Coombs in his grand summation. It should still all further arguments.

Before continuing with the manufacture of the Yorkshire Terrier, let us examine the description of these three dogs. Crab with a Terrier head, three-to four-inch coat and a long body with tan on legs and muzzle, was most likely a Clydesdale or Waterside Terrier. Kitty, with plenty of coat of a blue shade but destitute of tan on any part of the body, was no doubt a Paisley Terrier. Whittam's nameless bitch, with her racier build and tanned head and legs and a sort of grizzle back, was likely to have been out of Old English Terriers from the Manchester area.

The threads in the loom were set and the task of weaving ready to commence. Taking the offspring of these dogs, the early breeders began spinning their bloodlines. With interest in prize winning and competition growing in numbers, the shuttles' pace increased. The Yorkshire's complete development is so woven into the developing sport of showing dogs that it is necessary to know a little of how it began.

The first organized dog show ever held took place at Newcastle-upon-Tyne in 1859. In the following fourteen years, a number of shows for many breeds sprang up and, as in most things, practices crept in that emphasized the necessity of having some controlling authority.

In 1873, a group of gentlemen founded The Kennel Club in England. (The English kennel club is always called The Kennel Club.) They felt that their first priority should be the availability of recorded pedigrees. They set about compiling a Stud Book which contained the principal winners at the leading shows up to that date. It consisted of 4,027 dogs divided into forty breeds and varieties. It also contained "a code of rules for the guidance of dog shows, as well as for the manner in which field trials should be conducted." The dogs were divided into two groups, Non-Sporting and Sporting. Under Non-Sporting, the Yorkshire joined the select forty breeds as Broken-haired Scotch and Yorkshire Terriers and, since breeds were less clearly defined, some were registered as Toy Terriers (Rough and Broken-haired).

Prior to the first organized show in 1859, most of the exhibiting of dogs was haphazard. Usually the events were held in local public houses.

No one has yet been able to pin down the exact date when the showing of dogs in open competition started. Shows were mainly sponsored by publicans who, in their day, kept a dog pit, a rat pit, a boxed badger and a game bull around their establishments for the entertainment of their patrons and their dogs. Records of such dog exhibitions go back at least to 1844.

The Blue Anchor, kept by Jemmy Shaw, who was one of the first to realize the possibilities of dog exhibitions, ran an advertisement in 1849 for a show of the Toy Dog Club on May 27, 1849. The card reads:

> The Toy Dog Club holds their meetings every Thursday evening at Mr. J. Shaw's, Blue Anchor Tavern, Dunhill Row, Finsbury, London. Grand show next Sunday evening May 27th, Terriers, Spaniels, and Small Toy Dogs, when nearly every fancier in London, as well as several provincials now in town, will attend with their little beauties.

It is noteworthy that both Kitty and Crab's owners were publicans.

Naming of the Yorkshire

So many of the early influential fanciers who steamed ahead to produce the Yorkshire Terrier were from Yorkshire or its close environs that they finally gave this broken-haired Scotch Terrier a new name. In 1870 Angus Sutherland of Accrington, the then reporter for *The Field*, commenting on Mozart (a son of Huddersfield Ben) taking first prize in the variety class at Westmoreland said, "they aught no longer to be called Scotch Terriers but Yorkshire Terriers for having been so improved there."

Before leaving the Yorkshire Terrier with his new designation, it is impossible not to add Dr. Gordon Staples' comment from *Ladies' Dogs As Companions*, published in approximately 1876:

> Scotchmen are as a rule terribly proud even if they are terribly poor. They have the misfortune to be all born gentlemen, and have an innate scorn at aught that is weakly in plant or animal, aught that can bear and brave the storms that, for seven months of the year, sweep across the land of mountain and flood. Perhaps this is the reason why they will not be accountable for the beautiful little creature, which forms the subject of this Chapter. The Yorkshire Terrier, unlike the Skye is not,
>
> > "An Imp—hardy, bold and wild,
> > As best befits a mountain child."
>
> And so Scotland disowns it. The doggie must emigrate, and take another name. It is no longer the Scotch Terrier, nor the improved Scotch—as if anything really Scotch could be improved!—but the Yorkshire pure and simple. I don't know that the little animal has lost much by the change after all. There is no more genial hospitality to be found anywhere, than you meet in Yorkshire or Northern Lancashire. The very county itself with its rolling braes, its breezy green cliffs, its wimpling burn and heather—"mind ye o'hame." And just hear a Yorkshireman read "Tam O'Shanter" or the "Cottar's Saturday Night." I think I've found a good home for my pretty Blue and Tan.

Here in his new home of genial hospitality, the broken-haired Scotch Terrier merged with the broken-haired English Terrier. Crab, Kitty and Whittam's bitch, plus the offspring of rising young sires, had woven into whole the factors to produce a fixed breed. The pattern design was laid in the next years to produce a stud dog that could found a gold and blue bloodline.

The Early Breeders

One of the early fanciers most influential in setting the style was Peter Eden of Salford, Lancashire. He was the owner of many dogs, among which was Albert, a top winner from 1863 to 1865.

Mr. Inman and Mr. Burgess of Brighouse, Yorkshire, were active in the breed from 1867 through the early 1870s. Mr. Inman's earliest registered dog was Sandy (3651). Mr. Burgess judged the breed at Manchester in 1873, giving first in over nine pounds to Mrs. Jonas Foster's Bruce, first in under nine pounds to Mrs. Foster's Ben II, and first in under five pounds to her Cobden.

Mr. J. Spink helped to tailor the breed with his dogs. He owned Bounce, later sold to Mr. Ramsden, grandsire of immortal Huddersfield Ben. Mr. Spink also owned and registered (old) Sandy (3652), listed as under seven pounds. (Old) Sandy was the sire of Lady, Huddersfield Ben's dam.

(Old) Sandy, bred by Mr. Walshaw of Huddersfield, was by Haigh's Teddy, one of Crab's sons out of Walshaw's Kitty. He won first prize at Leeds in 1861. In the Kennel Club's first Stud Book, there are eight Sandys in the section for Broken-haired and Yorkshire Terriers and one Sandy, owned by Mrs. Foster, in the section for Toy Terriers (Rough and Broken-haired).

Huddersfield Ben

The design was ready and if Mr. W. Eastwood's (of Huddersfield) only claim to fame was the fact that he bred Huddersfield Ben, he would need no other. The only dog of his that is ever mentioned is his old Ben, though one feels that Lady—Ben's dam—should get some notice.

Huddersfield Ben (3612), born in 1865, was purchased by Mrs. Jonas (Mary A.) Foster, Lister Hill, Bradford, Yorkshire.

Ben has been given the title "Father of Broken-haired Scotch and Yorkshire Terriers," and the pedigrees of his progeny prove his right to it. He was no flyer, but the result of the work of the manufacturers of the breed. Through his well-planned breeding he was capable of producing all the best factors wanted in the breed. Mr. S. Jessop, in his book *The Yorkshire Terrier*, first published around 1900, says of Ben: "His merits as a show dog naturally found him in great request at the stud and luckily he possessed the rare trait of transmitting his virtues to his progeny. He was a great sire, one of those animals who make the history of the breed, and whose influence is apparent generations after the progenitor has passed away."

In reading Huddersfield Ben's pedigree the easiest thing to do is to ignore his dam's side, as Lady, his dam, was also the dam of his

Huddersfield Ben, born in 1865, was considered the founding father of the Yorkshire Terrier. He was owned by Mrs. Jonas Foster of Bradford, Yorkshire.

This head study of Huddersfield Ben is the only known painting of the breed patriarch done from life. This painting is now owned by the author.

sire, Mr. Boscovitch's dog. Thus he was the inbred offspring of a mother-son breeding.

Perhaps the most delightful way to give his pedigree is to let Dr. Gordon Staples do the job. In doing so, one must again wonder why a written record of 1876 has been so overlooked. But from *Ladies' Dogs As Companions* comes this tale from a gentleman who was—on occasion—Mrs. Foster's veterinarian:

> Now, of all the Yorkshire Terriers ever I saw, I think Huddersfield Ben was the best. Many of my readers doubtless remember this most beautiful prince of dogs, although it is now some few years since he was run over on the street and killed, he being then only in his prime. But he did not die before he had made his mark. Dog shows were not then quite so numerous as they are now, but nevertheless Ben managed to win seventy-four prizes ere his grand career was shortened on that unlucky 23rd of September (1871).
>
> "Pedigrees, few ladies I believe care to remember, so I shall not give Ben's in full, but be content with stating that he was bred by Mr. W. Eastwood, Huddersfield, and had the blood of Old Bounce in his veins, and his mother, Lady, was a daughter of Old Ben, a granddaughter of Old Sandy, and a great-granddaughter of Mr. W. J. Haigh's Teddy, and a great-great-granddaughter of Mr. J. Swift's Old Crab. I am the very worst genealogist in the world, so I cannot go back any further for fear of running on shore somewhere. Perhaps, though, Old Crab came over with the Conqueror—from Scotland you know.

So that Dr. Staples doesn't run aground, we'll fill in a few details. Mr. Boscovitch's dog (Ben's sire), whose name no one seems able to discover, was the result of Lady being bred to her grandsire Bounce, first owned by Mr. Spink, and then Mr. Ramsden. Mr. Watson in *The Book Of The Dog* describes Bounce as "Our illustration represents a very beautiful specimen of this sort, belonging to Mr. Spink of Bradford. He is the type of his class—a class deservedly popular with all admirers of rough Terriers, and in which he is famous." Going one step further, you find that Lady herself was produced by another mother-son breeding. Eastwood's Old Ben, her sire, was by Ramsden's Bounce bred to Young Dolly. Young Dolly was then bred to her sire Eastwood's Old Ben to produce Lady. One might say the material was very tightly woven. For if ever a dog was inbred, Huddersfield Ben can claim that honor. However, the results were worth the weaving of this producer of the blue and gold bloodlines.

Mrs. Jonas Foster set the fashion for the Yorkshire Terrier with the parading of her many homebred and purchased Yorkshires. She was not the only style-setter but, since she gained a great many prizes and her stud dogs were influential factors to the early American breeders, some of her development of the breed, we feel, should be included here. If you wish to learn more about these other early English fanciers, there are several English Yorkshire Terrier books that deal very sensibly with the subject.

Bradford was Mrs. Foster's choice for her kennel name and according to Mrs. Annie Swan, in her *Yorkshire Terrier Handbook*, Mrs. Foster was the first woman to judge at a Kennel Club show, Leeds in 1889. In addition to Yorkshire Terriers, she exhibited Toy Spaniels and black and tan Terriers. She showed Huddersfield Ben, winning seventy-four prizes with him. He produced many winning Yorkshires, among them Mr. Inman's Sandy, Hill's Sandy, Hirst's Peter, Miss Anderson's Mozart, Doctor Spark (also shown and registered as Charlie by a Mr. Stell), Mr. Mortimer's Edmond, and Lucas' Empress.

Mrs. Foster had winners sired by Huddersfield Ben in Little Kate, Bruce, Emperor, Sandy, Spring and Tyler. In addition to their winning, these dogs carried the ability to pass on their best factors.

Huddersfield Ben, after his unlucky death in 1871, like Crab, underwent the administrations of a taxidermist. Almost all of Ben's pictures are of the stuffed dog, which seems to have become the property of John Thorpe of Patriocroft, though it is doubtful if more than the glass case now survives.

Mrs. Foster had many winners and studs after Ben, one of which—Bradford Hero—had a great influence on the early American dogs. Mrs. Foster, in speaking of Hero's pedigree in 1885, said his blood "included all the best dogs for thirty-five years back, and they were all originally bred from Scotch Terriers." Bradford Hero was the grandsire of the first American bitch to gain her title.

Mrs. Foster owned Ch. Ted, a dog that was the sire or grandsire of a number of early American imports. She purchased Ted when he was four years old, at the Heckmondwike Show in 1887. Ch. Ted, bred by Mr. Fleming, weighed five pounds, and stood nine inches at his shoulder. His length, nose to set-on of tail was seventeen inches. He was said to be the shortest-backed dog in her kennel. Ted won 265 first prizes and in the year 1887, in ten months, won twenty-two first prizes, six special prizes of cups, gold medals and other prizes. He was the top dog in the breed for six years. Ted was by Bank's Young Royal, a grandson of Huddersfield Ben, out of Fleming's Annie, also a granddaughter of Ben's.

One consideration in the final production of the Yorkshire is the matter of whether the Maltese was bred into the Yorkshire or vice versa.

Quoting Virginia T. Leitch in *The Maltese Dog*, we find that "Mr. Robert Mandeville was the most celebrated breeder of Maltese in the 1860s. . . . In 1864, Birmingham established a class for Maltese and Mr. Mandeville won first and second prizes at this show with two dogs, each named Fido. Both these dogs were sired by a dog named Fido owned by Mr. Tupper, one being out of Mr. Mandeville's Lilly, and one out of his Fan. . . . No records are available as to the ancestry of Mr. Mandeville's Lilly or Fan, or of Mr. Tupper's Fido, or as to where they obtained their original stock."

Now checking over old records, Mr. Mandeville showed and won second at Islington in 1866 with Lilly and pups, and third with Prince. In 1863, Lilly was shown winning fourth as "*other Scotch Terrier*." Prince had been registered by Mr. Mandeville as a Broken-haired Scotch and Yorkshire Terrier, his number being 3640. Lilly was beaten at the London show of 1863, by Phin (3636), a son of (Old) Sandy out of a Huddersfield bitch. Lilly was not registered but the other four dogs in this class all were registered as Broken-haired Scotch and Yorkshire Terriers.

Mrs. Leitch also mentions as an early Maltese, Mr. T. Lee's Blondin (3593) and, again, this dog is registered in the Broken-haired Scotch and Yorkshire Terriers category. She also lists three of Mr. W. McDonald's dogs, two of which—Flora (3611) and Janet (3615)— were registered as Broken-haired Scotch and Yorkshire Terriers. The third dog, Jessie (3994), was registered as a Toy Terrier (rough and broken-haired). We finally find that Lady Gifford and Mrs. Bligh Monck are all reported as Maltese breeders, whereas they were all Yorkshire Terrier breeders, giving them up to continue in Maltese. In fact, Mrs. Monck's famous Maltese, Mopsy, whelped in 1865, listed as being out of Mr. McDonald's bitch sired by Mr. Mandeville's Fido (Tupper's Fido ex Mandeville's Lilly), would seem to have more claim to being a Broken-haired Scotch and Yorkshire Terrier than anything else. The answer to the question of what was what is, we presume,

Mrs. Foster's Ch. Ted.

Mrs. Foster's Little Tot, 1886.

that several of these dogs were, in fact, extremely silver Terriers carrying a strong dilution factor, which made them highly desirable to the Maltese breeders. These crossed facts are the only indication that Maltese and Yorkshires were interbred. Herein arose the myth that the Yorkie was descended from the Maltese.

The blue and gold silken Yorkshire caught the fancy of the Victorians. It was admired in the show ring as the best of "Fancy" Terriers. These fancy dogs with extra length of coat, of silkiness and evenness of color, brought on sales-producing extra pocket money to the men of Yorkshire. They became quite common as house pets in the Victorian way of life. In the carriage parade in Hyde Park, the Yorkie sat beribboned on a cushion at Milady's side, and was lifted in and out by a footman. The West End pet shops sold them as well as little patent leather boots, generally pale blue, which the little dogs wore to take their gentle exercise—while no doubt thinking up ways to sneak down the backstairs and kill a rat or two. However, neither the people in the pet shops, nor the purchasers and new fanciers in London, saw the progenitors from whom the Yorkie was manufactured, and, thus, his origins were forgotten and the factors used to produce him were woven into myths.

2

The American Pioneers

As THE STEAM ENGINE had provided power and work at the mills for the men of Yorkshire, so the steam engine provided and powered the ships that brought the Yorkshire Terrier across the Atlantic to the United States of America. The postwar America of 1870–1900 was a nation on the move. The first American-recorded Yorkshire Terrier was born in the last third of the nineteenth century in 1872, four years prior to America's first centennial in 1876.

The Yorkshire Terrier took the prim lace-curtained Victorian society by storm. Lawn tennis became fashionable in the 1870s, and so did the Yorkshire Terrier. It was being bred and shown up and down the East Coast prior to electric lights, refrigerators and telephones. Yorkshires were bred and shown before the Statue of Liberty came to Bedloe's Island, or the monument to Washington was finished. It took nearly seven days to travel coast-to-coast, but Yorkies were as popular in San Francisco and Los Angeles as the new rage of bicycling. They flourished in the lake ports of the Great Lakes as the new steel steam-powered carriers loaded wheat at the railheads from the newly opened territories to the barges on the Erie Canal. Yorkies were being bred in St. Louis while the great steam-driven side wheelers held sway, and Chicago had several breeders before the first skyscrapers were built.

By 1900 the nation had grown to include forty-five states and there were Yorkie breeders in twenty-two of them. They found their way to five more states by 1906.

There is no real proof of its being a frontiersman but it's possible to imagine that some little shaggy-haired, blue and tan ratting Terrier pioneered with an immigrant Yorkshireman, and there took up its duties as sod-house guardian and saloon rat-chaser. It did, we know, join at least one expedition using the new fad of photography.

The Yorkshire was originally the workingman's dog, but in the new country, the man who sold to the carriage trade in the Land-of-the-Free was certain to provide these fashionable dogs for his wealthy patrons, who so admired Victorian ways. That the Yorkie was a fashionable pet is shown by this quote from *The Practical Dogbook for Both the Professional and Amateur Fancier*, published in Philadelphia and copyrighted in 1884: "We now come to the breed that is preeminently the ladies' pet, and which by all persons ignorant of 'Doggy Lore' is constantly being confounded with the Scotch and the Skye. The Yorkshire is the handsomest of all long-haired terriers and makes a most bright, active and companionable indoor pet, and is, besides, the most fashionable dog today in this country, not excepting the Pug."

This is followed by the points of the breed and the prices for the breed which are given as: Males—$20 to $150, Females—$15 to $125; Puppies: Males—$15 to $25, Females—$10 to $20. And the Yorkshire was not just a fashionable pet, but a fashionable entrant in the breeding and showing of purebred dogs.

It has been said that the years pass and all that is left are memories, but in the case of the Yorkshire Terrier even the oldest breeder alive is too young to have memories of the start of the history of the breed in the United States. It is left for us, then, to remove the dust and search the old printed records for the early dogs and their breeders.

The first Yorkshire Terrier to have an AKC registered number was Butch (5396); the second was Daisy (5397). Both belonged to Charles Andrews, of Bloomington, Illinois.

The first Yorkie to actually appear in the AKC Stud Book was Belle, owned by Mrs. A. E. Godeffroy. She was first registered in the *National American Kennel Club Stud Book* in 1883. This Stud Book was taken over by the American Kennel Club in September 1884. Both Belle and Whitman's Gypsy appear in the AKC Stud Book before Andrews' dogs, but neither had an AKC registered number.

Belle was whelped in 1877, her sire, dam and breeder being

unknown—a circumstance which seems to have been a very common occurrence with the early dogs. On the other hand, a great many of the Yorkies entered at Westminster in 1878 carried the notation that the full pedigree was available from the owner, information that is unfortunately of little use to us over a century later. It does show that even at this early date these breeders knew the ancestors of their dogs.

The first bench show to be held in the United States was at Chicago on June 2, 1874. It was held by the Illinois State Sportsmen's Association. The second was held by the New York State Sportsmen's Association at Oswego, New York, on June 22, 1874. The third was at Mineola, Long Island, New York, October 7, 1874, and was considered the most successful of the three. The first bench show to be held by the Westminster Kennel Club in New York City was not held until three years later in 1877.

These early shows had their own rules, and even prior to the founding of the American Kennel Club dogs won championships. The qualifications for winning a title were that a dog must win four first prizes in the Open class, after which it was eligible to compete in the Challenge class. When a dog had won three first prizes in the Challenge class, it was a champion.

The AKC was founded September 17, 1884, in Philadelphia, and this method for winning a championship was continued, the only difference being that a dog now became a *Champion of Record*. This simply meant that the dog's championship was recorded in the AKC and published in AKC's official magazine. All dogs having already won their titles were listed providing they were still living at that time.

Mr. Coombs, early breeder and writer, reported in *The American Book of the Dog* that his Bradford Harry "is at present (1890) the only Champion of Record in America." It is noteworthy that he did not say he "is the *first* champion in the breed." To which dog that honor goes will, we are afraid, remain an unknown fact. We do know that Mr. and Mrs. Henry Kisteman's Hero did win in this class, and does appear in the certified AKC pedigree of Joker II (AKC No. 20,793) as Ch. Hero.

Ch. Hero was imported by the Kistemans from his breeder West Lucas, Blackburn, England. Kisteman's Hero was the winner of the over five pounds Champion class in both 1883 and 1884. In 1884, the first female appears as a winner of a Champion class, this being Kisteman's Crickie, winner of the under five pounds.

Among the winners elsewhere, Fred Sierp's Mash was the winner of the Champion class at San Francisco in 1888, '89, '91 and '92. The first female Champion of Record was the imported Minnie York, owned by Dr. N. Ellis Oliver of Chicago. Minnie won her title in 1893.

John Marriot, of New York City, is the oldest American breeder of whom any records are available. His Jack was the earliest dog of which records can be found. Jack was born in the United States in 1872, sired by Havelock, out of Jessie.

The entry at the Westminster Kennel Club show in New York in 1878 totaled thirty-three Yorkshire Terriers, divided into two classes by weight. Eighteen were shown in over five pounds, and fifteen were entered in under five pounds.

All the dogs entered at this 1878 show were born before 1877, the largest portion being Centennial babies born in 1876 or in 1875. Jack was valued, or could be claimed, for one thousand dollars, so apparently Mr. Marriot thought especially well of him.

Jack's sire, Havelock, appears to be the first stud dog that can be traced in American pedigrees, as another of his sons, "Jeff," appears as the sire of John Enright's (San Francisco) Sally VI, who was born some twenty years later.

During the late 1870s and up to 1889, Henry and Lena Kisteman of New York City were the most successful and active Yorkshire Terrier exhibitors. They exhibited almost twenty-five Yorkies during this peroid, as well as Toy Spaniels, Pugs, Field Spaniels, Japanese Spaniels and Toy Terriers. They started showing Yorkies with the New York show of 1877.

Ch. Hero, bred by Lucas, was the best of their dogs and first appeared in the Champion class for over five pounds in 1883—which he won. At the New York show of 1884, the Kistemans made a clean sweep in all four classes offered, winning both Championship classes and both Open classes.

Ch. Hero was the sire of Joseph Bell's Young Hero (purchased from the Kistemans in 1886), of Kisteman's Teddy (bred by Peter Cassidy) and of Jack III. Through this last dog, Ch. Hero's blood comes down into Yorkies being shown in the 1920s.

Little of the blood of these early breeders can be traced down to today. A few, with difficulty, come down to World War I but are then

An early American-bred Yorkshire Terrier that appeared on a post card, circa 1906.

Ch. Bradford Harry, the first American champion, was owned by P. H. Coombs.

Bradford Peter (*left*) and Bradford Ben, two early show dogs from Mrs. Foster's influential kennel. Ben was imported to the United States in 1898.

lost. Marriot and Kisteman's dogs' blood can be found, but tracing generation to generation quickly becomes a losing battle.

With Mrs. Fred Senn, of New York City, we come to a strain which *has* continued down to present time. Champions are being shown today that trace back to Mrs. Senn's dogs. Mrs. Senn showed her first Yorkie in 1878.

Those of you who are trying to finish your first champion can take heart from Mrs. Senn's persistence and love for the breed. It took from 1878 to 1905, exactly twenty-seven years, for her to finish her first Yorkie champion. This was Ch. Queen of the Fairies, who won her title in 1905 and was a top winner for the next four years, being shown from Boston to Washington, D.C., and as far west as Milwaukee. Mrs. Senn had shown eighty-five Yorkies up to this point. Ch. Senn Senn King, closely related to Ch. Queen of the Fairies, followed with his title in 1907.

With the birth of Mrs. Senn's Little Gem, the oldest American strain came into its own. Little Gem sired Little Gem II, who sired Little Gem III (as well as Ch. Queen of the Fairies). Little Gem III, in turn, sired Ch. Senn Senn King, who bred to Peter Menges' Little Fairy, produced Ch. Roxy II, owned by the Mengeses. Mrs. Anna B. Radcliffe bred her Lady Blue to Ch. Roxy II's son Ch. Prince II, and in 1917 Ch. Boy Blue was born. Ch. Boy Blue sired Gold Mount Lady Tena out of Mrs. Radcliffe's imported Ch. Lady Tena. Gold Mount Lady Tena, when bred to Gold Mount Gay Boy in 1924, produced Ch. Gold Blaze. Mrs. Radcliffe sold Ch. Gold Blaze and Gold Mount Lady Tena to Mrs. Harold Riddock of Detroit in 1926. Mrs. Riddock repeated this breeding and produced Gold Don, who was bred to May Blossom, a daughter of Ch. Gold Blaze and produced Miss June. Mrs. Riddock bred Miss June to her Canadian import, Ch. Bond's Byngo. (Mrs. Riddock had purchased this dog from Harry Draper of Toronto in 1928. Byngo was bred by Mrs. O. M. Bond of Canada.) This mating produced Mrs. Riddock's Ch. Byngo's Royal Masher, Mrs. Turnball's Ch. Byngo's Royal Tiny and Mrs. Goldie Stone's Ch. Petit Byngo Boy. The first two dogs were born in 1931 and Mrs. Stone's in 1930. The Petit blood continues down through many present-day American dogs.

In 1898, John Howard Taylor purchased a number of dogs from Mrs. Senn, and was active in the breed until around 1908. His most famous dog was Ashton Premier, bred by Mrs. Senn and purchased

Mrs. Ferdinand Senn's first American-bred title-holder Ch. Queen of the Fairies, a homebred that finished in 1905.

Mrs. Raymond Mallock's Ashton Premier, bred by Mrs. Ferdinand Senn.

After the turn of the century just as today, Yorkshire Terriers had their place in family portraits.

by Mr. Taylor in 1899. Mr. Taylor sold Premier to Mrs. Mallock in 1900, and she used this dog to illustrate the breed in her first book on Toy dogs.

Mrs. Senn's Brandy, sired Little Boy Blue, owned by Mrs. Michael Jennings. Thomas W. Mead's Meade's Daisy, a daughter of Little Boy Blue, was the great-granddam of Sam Baxter's Bobbie B.

Mrs. Senn's Senn Senn Kennels founded or contributed to almost all the kennels active from 1875 to 1909, and her dogs carried all the best English and American breeding Yorkshire Terriers. She was active for thirty-one years, and even eight years after ceasing to breed and show, she still appeared as an active member of the American dog fancy.

Mr. P. H. Coombs, of Bangor, Maine, was the man who first brought the breed to a position where it was a strong contender for top prizes. He was not only a breeder, but an exhibitor, a judge of the breed, a historian and authority on the breed. His article in Mr. Shield's *The American Book of the Dog* contains breeding, grooming and showing tips that are just as timely now as when they were written in 1890. Certainly the breed is indebted to him for collecting the history of the breed's beginnings.

In writing of the breed as it was in the 1870s and 1880s, Mr. Coombs says: "Unfortunately, at its first appearance at our shows, almost anything in the shape of a Terrier having a long coat, with some shade or effect of blue on the body, fawn or silver (more frequently the latter) colored head and legs, with tail docked and ears trimmed (cropped) was received and admired as a Yorkshire terrier by most everyone except the few competent judges; and the breed fashionable as it is, is still much neglected in this country for the reason that its care is not so well understood as that of many other breeds, and a good specimen soon loses its fine show condition by reason of lack of that regular and well directed care necessary to cultivate and keep the coat looking right."

Mr. Coombs' Ch. Bradford Harry (already noted as the first AKC Yorkie Champion of Record) was first shown in 1888 and won at Boston, New York, Troy, Lynn, Buffalo and New Bedford, winning nine first prizes in succession; and, in addition, he has made the remarkable record of which few dogs of any breed can boast—that of winning every special prize for which a Yorkshire Terrier was eligible to compete at the shows where he has appeared. In one show alone he won the specials for Best Yorkshire Terrier, Best Rough-Coated Terrier—any breed, and smallest dog in the show.

Ch. Bradford Harry was born May 16, 1885, being bred by W. Beal, England. Mr. Coombs gives his pedigree as: sire, Crawshaw's Bruce; dam, Beal's Lady; Bruce by Hodson's Sandy out of Patterson's Minnie; Sandy by Bateman's Sandy out of Venus; Bateman's Sandy by Spring out of Typsey; Venus by Music; Spring by Huddersfield Ben; Beal's Lady by Tyler out of lady; Tyler by Huddersfield Ben out of Bolton's Kitty; Kitty by Bolton's Wonder.

Both the first two American Champions of Record—Ch. Bradford Harry and Ch. Toon's Royal—were closely related, going directly back to Huddersfield Ben through three of his sons, Tyler, Spring and Mozart. Harry carried Tyler and Spring and Royal carried Mozart and Spring. Harry won first prizes at Newcastle and Darlington before leaving England.

That Ch. Bradford Harry was highly thought of is evident from the fact that his offspring were to be the foundation of many of the kennels across the country.

Charles N. Symonds, Salem, Massachusetts, and Mr. Toon, Sheffield, England, joined into partnership to sell dogs, and were active in many Terrier breeds. Assumedly, Mr. Toon picked the dogs and Mr. Symonds showed them here, selling them to prospective customers.

Mr. Symonds used two kennel names in his breeding and dealing in Yorkshire Terriers. They were Anglo-American Terriers, and the better known Northfield Yorkshire Kennels.

Symonds was a Yorkie breeder and probably did breed other Terriers. He started in 1885 and continued for around ten years. Among his imports were Prince A. I., Fishpool Gem and Ch. Minnie York. All were resold to buyers here.

Mr. Symonds won a title with Ch. Toon's Royal, showing him in both the United States and Canada. Royal (bred by J. Hamilton of England) was sired by Mrs. Troughear's Dreadnaught, a full brother to Eng. Ch. Conqueror. Royal was first shown in 1890, and won well in 1891–1892.

In 1891, Dr. N. Ellis Oliver purchased Minnie York from Symonds and Toon, finishing her championship in 1895, which made her the first female Champion of Record in the breed. Ch. Minnie York was sired by Duke of Leeds, a son of Dreadnaught out of Minnie, a daughter of Mrs. Foster's Eng. Ch. Bradford Hero.

Considering traveling conditions of the early 1890s, Dr. Oliver was certainly a determined exhibitor. He won firsts with Dick York, Nellie York and Ch. Minnie York in Omaha, Nashville, Denver and Detroit in 1892 and 1893. By 1898, Dr. Oliver was exhibiting as far away as Dallas, taking first with Pansy York.

Mrs. George S. Thomas, wife of the well-known judge and Terrier fancier, started in Yorkies in 1896 and did a great deal of importing, showing the imports and reselling the dogs. In *The New Book of the Dog* (1911) by Robert Leighton, the author gives Endcliffe Muriel, Midge and Margery as her best homebreds with Endcliffe Merrit as her best import. Merrit was originally imported by J. J. Holgate and shown under his English-registered name of Persimmon. Mr. Holgate imported Crown Prince as well as showing both dogs in 1900 at the New York show, winning first with Persimmon and Reserve with Crown Prince. Mrs. Thomas purchased both dogs, changing their names to Endcliffe (the Thomas' kennel name) Merrit and Mentor. Endcliffe Merrit (formerly Persimmon) was by Eng. Ch. Merry Mascot. Mr. Leighton's description of Mascot reads: "He is five inches high at the shoulder and weighs five lbs. His head and expression (his ears being cropped) are reputed to be very Terrier-like; his eyes small and dark; body low to the ground, and perfectly level top and carriage of tail erect. Tan very deep and rich, with one of the best blue backs ever exhibited. Coat perfectly straight and of grand texture, and his action unexcelled." If the height and weight are correct as given, we would have to assume he was very long backed. Endcliffe Muriel and Margery were sold to Mrs. Senn in 1905.

Mrs. Raymond Mallock was considered an authority on the Yorkshire and was the author of several books on the breed including *Toy Dogs*, published in 1907 by Dogdom Publishing Company, and *The Up-to-Date Pekingese and all other Toy Dogs,* published by herself.

In *Toy Dogs*, Mrs. Mallock illustrates the breed with Ashton Premier. In the *Up-to-Date Pekingese*, he is listed as Ashton-More Premier. In the United States, Mrs. Mallock used the kennel name "Ashton," but on moving to England she had to change the kennel name to "Ashton-More" as Ashton was already being used by Mesdames Sheard and Walton.

Mrs. H. H. (Flo) Teschemacher was the most active breeder in the St. Louis area from 1891 to 1910. She imported several English dogs and bought a number of top American-bred winners.

Of Mrs. Teschemacher's dogs, Boy can be traced down to present time. Boy was originally shown as Rosedale Teddy, and why she chose to register him just Boy rather than the fancier name gives room for all sorts of ideas. Boy was the grandsire of Gaby Keller, the great-granddam of Boots, bred by Mrs. Beck, and acquired by Mrs. Goldie Stone in the 1930s. Through Mrs. Stone's dogs the line continued into a number of kennels of the late 1930s, coming on down to the present time.

In 1895, L. Cullen purchased Endcliffe Maud and Model from Mrs. Thomas who had imported them. Mr. Cullen, in 1898, imported Eng. Ch. Bradford Ben and Bradford Sultan from Mrs. M. A. Foster. Bradford Ben was one of Mrs. Foster's top winners and was pictured in several books as an example of the breed.

Fred W. Sierp, was the pioneer breeder on the West Coast. His first dog, Mash, was born in 1883, and was good enough to still be winning the Champion class at the age of nine years in 1892 at San Francisco.

Mrs. E. B. Grace started breeding in 1893 when she bought Sis from Mr. Sierp. She showed in both San Francisco and Los Angeles. Besides from Mr. Sierp, she bought Sally VII from John Enright of San Francisco. Sally VII was a great-granddaughter of Marriot's Jack through her sire Prince.

In 1896 Mrs. Grace entered Sally VII at San Francisco, but the listing of awards in this show catalogue say "Dead" beside her name. We're not sure whether that was the judge's opinion, or an actual fact. Mrs. Grace continued breeding until 1900.

In 1893, a Yorkshire Terrier—Topsey—was registered to Edward Darcourt of Diaz, Mexico—first of the breed in that country.

3

The New Century Breeders

IN THE GOLDEN interlude between 1900 and the First World War, the comfortable time bridging the end of "the good old days" and the arrival of modern times, there were sixty-five breeders of Yorkshire Terriers in America.

Yorkies were being bred all across the country. Railroads criss-crossing the nation were utilized in the exchange of bloodlines. The new transportation, the tin lizzie, made it easier to travel and to purchase new stock, or to exhibit at the ever-increasing number of dog shows.

In 1905, two years after the Wright brothers had flown the first flying machine, the first American-bred Yorkie gained her title. Who in that day would have believed that there would come a time when the "silly contraptions" would be flying dogs to shows to gain their championships?

The Early Decades

Hunslet, owned by Mrs. Emanuel Battersby, was founded in 1907 with the importation of Hunslet Zena, who became a champion in

1909. Zena carried Ch. Ted on her sire's side and it was from her that Mrs. Battersby took her kennel name.

In 1913 Mrs. Battersby imported Little Shannon Jr., winning his title in 1915. In 1921, Mrs. Battersby imported Ch. Conran Toy (Eng. Ch. Harpuhey Hero ex Lady Gay). He sired Ch. Rochdale Queenie and Ch. Rochdale Playmate (ex Hunslet Lady Ramsey—a granddaughter of Ch. Little Shannon Jr.) who were the foundation bitches of Mr. and Mrs. John Shipp's Rochdale Yorkshires.

Ch. Rochdale Queenie's daughter Olinda Queen was the great granddam of Goldie Stone's Ch. Petit Byngo Boy and Mrs. Riddock's Ch. Byngo Royal Masher.

Mrs. Michael Jennings (J's) was active for only eight years but her breeding was the connecting link to Mrs. Senn's line. Her Ch. Little Boy Blue (Senn's Brandy II) was the great granddam of Bide-a-Wee, the bitch Sam Baxter started his line with in 1920.

Mr. and Mrs. Peter Menges purchased Molly J (Ch. Little Boy Blue) from Mrs. Jennings in 1912. Her Little Fairy, purchased from Mrs. Senn was the dam of Ch. Roxy II who won his title in 1913.

Ch. Roxy II (Ch. Senn Senn King) sired the first champion littermates in the breed.—Ch. Billy and Ch. Prince II.

Mr. and Mrs. James Dwyer purchased Ch. Prince II and his son Ch. Boy Blue II was the foundation of Anna Radcliffe's Gold Mount line. Mr. and Mrs. George Peabody started Douro in 1904 with the English import, Masterpiece (a grandson of Halifax Marvel).

The Peabodys showed until the start of World War I. During this period they imported Douro Chief (Eng. Ch. Armley Fritz) who gained his American title and became the top winner in the United States during 1909–1910. Ch. Armley Necco (Armley Toff), the sire of F. L. Parnham's Ch. Nemo and the Thomas Lomasney's Ch. Sporting Lady.

Mr. Peabody was a delegate to the American Kennel Club for the first Yorkshire Terrier Club of America, started around 1912. This club, according to AKC records, held its first licensed specialty in New York on February 12, 1918. Unfortunately no records remain of the winner of this show.

Mrs. Anna Bell (Madero) purchased Ch. Douro Saucy Bob and Ch. Douro Wee Dolly as the foundation of her kennel in 1914. Mr. William Cummings' English import Ch. Teddy Boy (a grandson of Armley Fritz) sired John Kenyon's Can. Ch. Haslingden Jack Oh Boy.

Mr. Kenyon sold Jack to Mr. and Mrs. Harry Smith in 1922 and

Ch. Duoro Wee Dolly, owned by Anna Bell, Madero Kennels, and bred by Mr. and Mrs. George Peabody.

Ch. Rochdale Queenie, owned by Mr. and Mrs. John Shipp and bred by Mrs. Emanuel Battersby, was selected BB at the Westminster KC 1925.

the Smiths carried on Haslingden after Mr. Kenyon retired. Jack was the great-grandsire of Mrs. Riddock's Ch. Bond's Byngo.

During the 1920s and the 1930s much breeding activity took place between Canadian and American breeders; without this pattern Yorkies in North America would have been in serious trouble.

Mrs. W. A. Beck must be considered one of the Yorkshire's major breeders. She bred from 1907 until 1938. Her dogs carried the blood of every top American dog starting with Mr. P. H. Coombs' Ch. Bradford Harry and continuing through Mrs. Riddock's Ch. Bond's Byngo.

Mrs. Beck purchased the English import, Ch. Clayton Wee Marvel in 1917. He sired Ch. O'Boy and was the grandsire of Mrs. Beck's top brood bitch So Long Letty. Letty was the dam of Mrs. Goldie Stone's bitch Boots (Pellon Sir Dandy) which she purchased in 1933.

Mrs. Anna Radcliffe started Gold Mount in 1914 and remained active till 1926.

Lady Blue, was a granddaughter of L. Cullen's English import Chelsea King. King was a great-grandson of Huddersfield Ben. Lady Blue was the dam of Gold Mount Gay Boy, a dog that played a major part in Mrs. Riddock's Olinda line.

Mrs. Radcliffe's English import Ch. Little Babs (The King's Own ex Peace Baby) won the breed at Westminster in February 1921. At that show, Babs is listed in the catalogue as being for sale for $200. After this win she no longer carried a price tag in her catalog entry at the Westchester show held in the fall of the same year.

Mr. and Mrs. William Thompson established Gatenby in 1913 and continued active until 1942. Mrs. Thompson was President of the second breed club—The Yorkshire Terrier Association started around 1919 and it faded away around 1924. Their top dogs were English imports: Ch. Gatenby's St. Wilfred's King (a grandson of Ch. Armley Fritz) and Ch. Gatenby's Armley Dick.

The Thompsons won titles on at least six, all of which were based on the English lines of Armley and Pellon. The imported Gatenby Bobs was sold to Sam Baxter in 1925 as his foundation stud.

From Armistice to Armistice (1920 to 1946)

In the two decades from 1900 to 1920, forty-five dogs won their titles. However the cessation of imports during World War I and the

Yorkshires shared the fun and good times during the roaring twenties as they always have and still do. The breed has always enjoyed the favor of the style conscious. *Jeanne Grimsby*

loss of breeders due to the problems associated with war, reduced the number of breeders at the end of the war to only eight American and two Canadian breeders.

Mr. and Mrs. John Shipp (Rochdale) took over all of Mrs. Battersby's Hunslet's dogs in 1924, as well as all of Mrs. John McHugh's Athaclee dogs.

Ch. Rochdale Queenie (Ch. Conran Toy) won her title in 1923, and was the dam of Ch. Rochdale Queen of the Toys and Ch. Rochdale Honey. The last two were sired by Am. & Can. Ch. Haslingden Dandy Dinty. Ch. Rochdale Queen of the Toys was the Shipp's top winner placing third in the Group at Westminster in 1935.

Andre Patterson started in 1920 and retired in 1937. He purchased from Harry Smith Am. & Can. Ch. Haslingden Dandy Dinty (Can. Ch. Little Briton ex Haslingden Jewel) which was the first Yorkie to sire five champions, as well as Sam Baxter's Bobbie B.

Dandy Dinty was third in the Group at Westminster in 1934. Mr Patterson had placed fourth in 1933 with Earl Byng, a full brother to Mrs. Riddock's Ch. Bond's Byngo.

Mrs. Harold Riddock (Olinda) was probably one of the breed's greatest enthusiasts, a breeder who carried on at a time when the Yorkshire Terrier was at its lowest ebb in popularity. She started in 1924 when she took over Anna Radcliffe's Gold Mount dogs. Her stock formed the foundation for Mrs. Stone's Petit; Harry Smith's Haslingden, and the Arthur Mills' Millbarry lines.

Ch. Gold Blaze (Gold Mount Gay Boy ex Gold Mount Lady Tena) was the sire of May Blossom (ex Olinda Queen) owned by Goldie Stone. Gold Mount Gay Boy's son, Gold Don was the sire of Miss June (ex May Blossom) also owned by Mrs. Stone.

The Group winner Am. & Can. Bond's Byngo (Can. Ch. Lord Byng ex Cave Girl) sired Mrs. Riddock's Am. & Can. Ch. Byngo's Royal Masher and Mrs. Stone's Ch. Petite Byngo Boy. Miss June was the dam of both prior to her sale to Mrs Stone. Royal Masher placed in ten Toy Groups in 1935.

Can. & Am. Ch. Bond's Byngo, bred by Mrs. O. M. Bond of Canada, was purchased from Harry Draper (Walkley), an outstanding Canadian breeder.

Mr. Draper attended his first Specialty in England in 1890 and his knowledge of the breeders and early dogs, as well as his knowledge

Ch. Haslingden Dandy Dinty, owned by Andre Patterson, was a top winner during the mid 1930's.

Ch. Little Babs, owned by Anna Radcliffe, was BB at Westminster in 1921.

It would be difficult to imagine any contemporary fancier exhibiting a Yorkshire, making a most coveted win then chucking the winner in a coat pocket at the end of the day and heading home. But in 1937, after winning BB at Westminster, that's just what the redoubtable Sam Baxter did with his Bobbie B, IV, rosettes and all! *And not a wrapping in sight.*

of breeding was overwhelming. He was of great help to us and we will always be thankful to have known him. Mr. Draper came to Canada in 1913 and remained an active breeder until 1954. His best-known dog was the Group winner, Can. Ch. Petite Lord Byngo of Walkley (Ch. Petite Byngo Boy) bred by Goldie Stone and purchased in 1948.

Sam Baxter had been Andrew Carnegie's coachman until he retired. He purchased his first Yorkie for two dollars and fifty cents. It was a little dog he saw perched beside the driver of an ash and dust cart.

His first show dog was the English import purchased from the Thompsons, Gatenby Bobs (Armley Little Bobs).

Bobbie B (Ch. Haslingden Dandy Dinty) was the start of a line of winners all with the same name.

Bobbie B III (Bobbie B II ex BeeBe—a Gatenby Bobs daughter) won third in the Group at Westminster in 1936. Bobbie B IV won the breed there in 1937. There was also a Bobbie B V and VI.

Mr. Baxter never finished a champion although he won points on a number of his dogs. He was president of the third breed club in 1937—The Yorkshire Terrier Club of America, which again faded out with the advent of World War II.

Mr. and Mrs. Henry Shannon started breeding in 1927 after emigrating from England. The Shannons imported many dogs and on those they bred and showed they either used no kennel name or used the English kennel names of Harringay and Mendham, and left some of the naming to the new owners. Hence one has to check twice to trace their breeding.

Madame-Be-You (Harringay Quality Boy—The Shannon's top stud dog ex Miss Why Be You—both imports) was sold to Goldie Stone in 1930 and was the first bitch to produce five champions.

The start of Goldie Stone's Petite line was the point at which the breed began its climb to its present popularity.

Her combining of the older American and Canadian lines produced the greatest number of top winners and champions ever produced by one kennel up to that time.

Mrs. Stone saw her first Yorkie, "Mike," in 1908 in a vaudeville act that was on the same stage bill as she and he performed a tightwire act.

In 1931, eighteen years later, her desire to raise Yorkies became fulfilled when she purchased, at six weeks, from Mrs. Riddock the

Am., Can. Ch. Bond's Byngo, owned by Mrs. Harrold Riddock, was a top winner during 1929 and 1930.

Ch. Petit Magnificent Prince, owned and bred by Goldie Stone, was the first American-bred Yorkshire to win an all breed BIS in the United States. The three-pound topper accomplished this feat in 1954 at three years old.

This 1941 photo shows Mrs. Goldie Stone with her Ch. Petit Sweet Boy and Ch. Petit Wee Gaffer.

Mrs. Paul Durgin with the Toy Group winners Ch. Durgin's Mickey and Ch. Durgin's Pilot and Pilot's sister, Ch. Durgin's Pansy.

future Ch. Petite Byngo Boy who was to become the top-winning Yorkshire Terrier during the early 1930s winning three Groups and siring five champions.

Ch. Petit WeeWee won fourteen Toy Groups; Ch. Petite Tiny Trinket won four Groups and Ch. Petit Baby Jill won seven Groups— all three were sired by Ch. Petite Byngo Boy.

Ch. Petit Magnificent Prince was the first American-bred to win Best in Show which he did in 1954. He also won three Toy Groups. Prince was the last dog shown by Mrs. Stone.

Mrs. Fred Rice (Bee's) purchased her first Yorkie in 1899 and showed her last one in 1966 at the age of eighty-nine. Her first champion was Ch. Bee's Super Boy (Ch. Fritty ex Ch. June Rose). His dam was a daughter of Colonel John Rose's Can. Ch. Little Jetsom, who was the winner in Canada of three Bests in Show and nineteen Groups in the early 1930s.

Ch. Hifalutin, CD (Charlotte's Sensation ex Gwen-Mar's Lady Allure) bred by Mrs. Rice, and owned by Pearl Kincarte, sired five champions.

Mrs. Rice's Ch. Gwen-Mar's Bitty Britches (Ch. Millbarry Sho Sho ex Ch. Lady Anne Plushbottom, a Ch. Fritty daughter) won two Groups and her Little Wee Won was Best of Breed at the second sanction match of the YTCA in 1953.

Helen Palmer (Vermont) started breeding Yorkshire Terriers in 1922 and continued until 1960. Ch. Minute Man of Tewae was her top winner and was a double grandson of Bobbie B III.

Mary and Arthur Mills started Millbarry in 1936. In 1938 after a vacation in England, the Mills returned with three dogs that were destined to play a major part in the history of the breed. These were Chs. Fritty, Miss Wynsum and Suprema.

Ch. Miss Wynsum (Sunny Boy ex Bronte Connie) won eight Toy Groups including the Group at Westminster in 1938.

Ch. Suprema (Eng. Ch. Supreme ex Little Bess) won two Groups and sired seven champions including Group winners Kay Finch's Ch. Pretty Please and the Mills' Ch. Millbarry Sho Sho.

Ch. Suprema was purchased by Gwen and Martin Krakeur (Gwen-Mar) in 1942. In 1945 the Krakeurs purchased Sho Sho, which was the second Yorkie to win the Toy Group at Westminster. He achieved this while still the property of the Mills. Sho Sho won twelve Groups and sired three champions including Kay Finch's (Crown Crest) Ch. Tidbit.

Ch. Miss Wynsum, owned by Mr. and Mrs. Arthur Mills, was an English import and the winner of eight Toy Group firsts including Westminster 1938.

Ch. Suprema, owned by Gwen and Martin Krakeur and imported from England by Mr. and Mrs. Arthur Mills. This notable dog won two Toy Groups and was the sire of seven champions.

Ch. Fritty was another celebrated import of the Arthur Mills. A winner of ten Toy Groups, he was also a successful sire. He was first owned by the actress Mary Carlisle and ultimately by Mrs. Fred Rice.

Ch. Fritty (Broad Lane Binkie ex Blue Bubbles) won ten Toy Groups. In 1954 Fritty was voted the mascot of the current Yorkshire Terrier Club of America and was used as the model for the Club's official pin. Fritty sired the Group winners Lily Harris' Ch. Frittlaria and Ethel Smith's Ch. Blue Knight.

In 1950, the Mills imported Ch. Gay Princess of Cayton (Master Midget ex Little Miss Thistledown). Princess won several Groups and might have won many more had she not died from an overdose of anesthetic during minor surgery. In all Millbarry bred or owned twenty champions.

Crown Crest, owned by Kay Finch, in Corona Del Mar California, started in 1941 with breeding based on the Millbarry dogs. Her Ch. Tidbit, a son of Ch. Millbarry Sho Sho was a Group winner and sired four champions. His sons Ruby Bixler's Ch. Acama Quite A Bit sired five champions and Nell Fietinghoff's Ch. Tiddle-wink sired eight champions.

Ch. Millbarry Sho-Sho, bred by the Arthur Mills and owned by the Krakeurs, established an outstanding record in the early forties. His wins included BIS at the prestigious Progressive Dog Club (Toy breeds only) in 1943 and Best Toy at the Westminster KC in 1944.

Ch. Rugene King Corkyson, owned and bred by Ruth and Gene
Fields.

Ch. Penney's Touch of Class, owned and bred by Alberta Walsh, was
sired by Ch. Rugene King Corkyson.   *Missy Yuhl*

4

In Our Time

THE PERIOD since World War II has seen the Yorkshire Terrier become ''popular.'' The breed has risen from ninety-sixth place in 1942 to fourteenth in 1991.

The Yorkshire's popularity is fully understandable to we who are enamored with the breed. This popularity should, however, be of concern to all fanciers as it can have devastating effects. Quality, not quantity is what makes for the health and advancement of any breed.

We all owe an immeasurable debt to those breeders in the United States, Canada and Great Britain who maintained breeding stock through wartime conditions.

The 1990s find the Yorkshire secure in the number of its active breeders, the quality of the dogs and, with jet age transportation, able to reach any breeding stock, or destination here or abroad in a matter of hours. An undreamed-of circumstance by those breeders who came before.

From after the Second World War until the present the breed in the United States has been completely influenced by English and Irish imports. All our contemporary bloodlines are based on the sires from these families. Our breed would not exist as we now know it without them. They are the foundations of all of today's winners and producers.

They and their offspring, whether many or few, are the gene pool on which all our present breeding is based.

Those sires are:

Eng. & Am. Ch. Buranthea's Doutelle
Eng. & Am. Ch. Don Carlos of Progresso
Ch. Finstal Royal Icing
Irish Ch. Gleno Credit Card
Ch. Golden Fame
Kelpie's Belziehill Dondi
Ch. Little Sir Model
Irish & Am. Ch. Peter of Nordlaw
Pretoria Action
Eng. & Am. Ch. Progress of Progresso
Ch. Quarnhill Fusspot
Ch. Star Twilight of Clu-Mor
Ch. Streamglen Luna Star
Ch. Toy Clown of Rusklyn
Ch. Wenscoe's Whizzaway of Tzumiao

Mrs. Paul Durgin of St. Paul, Minnesota, started in Yorkshires in 1940. In 1951 she imported from Ireland Pretoria Action (Eng. & Ir. Ch. Twinkle Star of Clu-Mor ex Connie of Adelaide.) Action's daughter, Caroline of Clonmel was the dam of three litter sisters who appear in all Clarkwyn breeding and the pedigrees of many Wildweir dogs. They were Clarkwyn Debutante, Wildweir Butterscotch and Wildweir Lollipop.

Iola Suhr Dowd, El Monte, California, imported Ir. & Amer. Ch. Peter of Norlaw. Peter's sire, Little Comet of Clu-Mor was also the sire of Ch. Twinkle Star of Clu-Mor. Bred to the English import, Gayways' Tim's Mite he sired Group winner Ch. Patoot's Maryetta and Patoot's Jonathon.

Jonathon was purchased by Allen and Stella Davis of the Ramon Yorkshires in Palm Springs, California. Here he sired seven champions, including Group and Specialty winner Ch. Little Sir Chuck of Ramon, Group winners Ch. Lilly of Ramon and Ch. Rugene's King Corky.

Rugene was started by Ruth and Gene Fields in 1951. Ch. Rugene's King Corky sired seven champions. His son Ch. Rugene's King Corkyson won five Groups, one Specialty and sired six champions including Alberta Walsh's Ch. Penney's Touch of Class. Mrs. Walsh started her line in 1966 in Paradise, Arizona. Touch of class was a Group winner and the sire of twenty-three champions. His son, Ch. Paradise That Special Touch (ex Ch. Barbee's Cinderella Paradise—a daughter of Ch. Cede Higgens) won two Groups. Touch of Class' son, Linda McClanahan's Ch. Lottaluv's Sky's the Limit is the winner of six Groups and one Specialty. Sky is bred and owned by Linda McClanahan, Scottsdale, Arizona.

In 1960 Myrtle Young, of Arlington, New Jersey, imported Eng. & Am. Ch. Don Carlos of Progresso (Eng. Ch. Martywyn's Wee Teddy) sire of eight champions—five American and three English.

The same year Jim Nickerson and Bud Priser of Windamere Yorkshires in Muncie, Indiana, imported the Don Carlos son Ch. Progress of Progresso (ex Ch. Coulgorm Chloe). Progress was a Best in Show winner in England, America and Canada. He won eleven Groups and sired fourteen champions including Ch. Gaytonglen Teddy of Mayfair. In all, Windamere owned or bred nine Group winners.

Kelpie's Belziehill Dondi was born in the United States, although his dam was imported in whelp from Scotland by Mildred Hornbrook of Ithaca, New York, in 1958. Mrs. Hornbrook owned the Danby Belziehill line. Dondi sired sixteen champions including four Group winners—Grace Getz's Ch. Gaybrook Steiff Toy, Mayfair-Barban's Chs. Danby Belziehill Raindrop, Danby Belziehill Amanda and Ch. Dandy Diamond of Mayfair.

Mrs. Hornbrook's imported Daisy of Libertyhill produced nine champions all sired by Dondi. Daisy's daughter Danby Belziehill Abigail produced nine champions and Daisy's granddaughter, Danby Belziehill Anya also produced nine champions.

Anne Seranne started Mayfair in 1960 and the name became Mayfair-Barban in 1966 when Barbara Wolferman became her partner. Miss Seranne died in 1988, and since then Miss Wolferman has carried on the line in joint ownership with Peter D'Auria.

Mayfair-Barban in Newton, New Jersey, has owned or bred seventy-three champions, which include six Best in Show winners, twenty-one Group and three Specialty winners.

Ch. Dandy Diamond of Mayfair was by Kelpie's Belziehill Dondi out of Ch. Topsey of Tolestar who was a Group winner and was purchased from David and Nancy Lerner (Renrel) who had imported her. Dondi's granddam, Candy of Hintonwood, Topsey's dam and Wildweir Sorreldene Salome were all litter sisters, their sire, Eng. Ch. Blue Symon was a son of Ch. Golden Fame. Diamond sired thirteen

Kelpie's Belziehill Dondi, owned by Mildred Hornbrook, was a sire of 16 champions.

Ch. Gaytonglen Teddy of Mayfair, owned by Anne Seranne and Barbara Wolferman and bred by Doris Craig, was a multiple BIS and Specialty winner and the sire of 26 champions.

Eng., Am., Can. Ch. Progress of Progresso, owned by Bud Priser and Jim Nickerson, was a BIS winner in three countries and the sire of 14 champions.

Ch. Mayfair-Barban Loup de Mer, owned and bred by Anne Seranne and Barbara Wolferman, was a highly successful show dog as well as a noteworthy sire. He is shown here with his handler, Wendell J. Sammet.

Ch. Mayfair-Barban Jamoca, owned by Doreen Hubbard and bred by Anne Seranne and Barbara Wolferman. This top-producing show dog is pictured with his owner. *Pierre Wibaut*

Ch. Hydcroft Thousands Cheer, owned and bred by Janet Heid (*far right*), is shown scoring a Yorkshire Terrier Club of America Specialty Best under the late Richard Hammond, handler Greg Larson. Trophy presenter is Dorothy Truitt.

champions including Ch. Trivar Bon Vivant and Ch. Mayfair Oddfella, a winner of twelve Groups.

In 1967, Ch. Gaytonglen Teddy of Mayfair (Eng. & Am. Ch. Progress of Progresso ex Gaytonglen Golden Tammie) was purchased from Doris Craig. Teddy was the winner of four Bests in Show, twenty-six Groups, two Specialties and he sired twenty-six champions.

His daughter, Ch. Mayfair-Barban Yam N' Yelly was a Best in Show winner. His son, Ch. Mayfair-Barban Mocha Mousse was a Group winner and sired eleven champions including Ch. Danby Belzie-hill Raindrop Yorkboro's Ch. Mayfair-Barban Jamoca and Nina McIn-tyre's (Chelsa-Nimar) Ch. Mayfair-Barban Poulet dam of four champions.

Ch. Devanvale Jack in the Box was purchased from Lynne Devan (Devanvale) in 1973 and sired seven champions. The Jack in the Box son, Ch. Mayfair-Barban Loup de Mer won eight Bests in Show, forty-seven Toy Groups firsts and was the sire of five champions. Loup de Mer's son, Ch. Danby Belziehill Oscar sired five champions. Oscar's son, Ch. Mayfair-Barban Yummy sired five champions including the Group winner, Ch. Yorkboro Putting on the Ritz and top producer Ch. Yorkboro All Time High.

Yummy's full brother, Ch. Mayfair-Barban Yohoo was a Group winner and sire of eight champions. His son Ch. Mayfair-Barban Quinnat won five Bests in Show, fifty-six Groups and sired eleven champions. Quinnat's son, Ch. Hydecroft Thousands Cheer, owned by Janet Heid won five Groups and has sired ten champions. Yohoo's son, Ch. Mayfair-Barban Verikoko won six Bests in Show, twenty-seven Groups and one Specialty.

Ch. Mayfair-Barban Lyonnaise won three Toy Groups and Ch. Mayfair-Barban Woodruff has won a Group.

Mrs. Doreen Hubbard (Yorkboro) started in Canada in 1964, relocating to to Marysville, Washington, in 1979. Forty-eight champions including four Best in Show winners, ten Group winners and four Specialty winners have been bred or owned by Yorkboro.

Ch. Mayfair-Barban Jamoca purchased in 1973 was the top Yorkie in Canada 1975–1976 and won the Canadian YTC Specialty. He sired ten champions.

Jamoca's daughter, Ch. Camelot's Robin of Yorkboro was the top-winning Yorkie in Canada in 1977–1978, winning two Bests in Show.

Ch. Yorkboro Crimson and Clover (Jamoca ex Oaksaber Gold

Am., Can. Ch. Yorkboro Crimson and Clover, bred and owned by Doreen Hubbard, is a daughter of Ch. Mayfair-Barban Jamoca. *Carl Lindemaier*

Am., Can. Ch. Yorkboro One Step Closer (Ch. Mayfair-Barban Quinnat ex Ch. Yorkboro Crimson and Clover), owned and bred by Doreen Hubbard, is a Specialty and all-breed BIS winner and successful producer. *Missy Yuhl*

Am., Can. Ch. Yorkboro Colour By Number, owned and bred by Doreen Hubbard, is a son of Am., Can. Ch. Yorkboro One Step Closer. *Carl Lindemaier*

Confetti—dam of four champions) produced twelve champions. Almost all Yorkboro dogs are descended from her.

Her son Ch. Yorkboro One Step Closer (by Ch. Mayfair-Barban Quinnat) won one Best in Show, three Groups, one Specialty and sired seven champions. One Step Closer's son Ch. Yorkboro Colour By Number won one Best in Show and three Groups, another son Ch. Russon's New Year Dream has sired seven champions.

Ch. Yorkboro Step By Step, One Step Closer's brother, sired seven champions including Group and Specialty winner Yorkboro's Ch. Hyline No Deposit No Return.

Clover's daughter, Ch. Yorkboro All Time High is the dam of six champions including Natlee Robert's Ch. Yorkboro My Main Man, winner of one Best in Show and the Fiegelsons Group winner Ch. Yorkboro Great Balls of Fire. Clover was also the dam of Specialty and Group winner Ch. Yorkboro Stop The Music, Ch. Yorkboro Putting on the Ritz and Ch. Yorkboro Follow The Leader, sire of seven champions.

Jamoca's son Jay Ammon's Ch. Montclair The Devil Himself has sired forty-four champions including Ch. Yorkboro My Main Man.

Sharon and Ed McAdam of Mt. Vernon, Washington (Firacres), purchased Ch. Jofre's Castle in the Sky from Jofre Yorkshires in 1990. Castle in the Sky was bred by Wanda Murphy. His sire, Ch. Castle Song Sung Blue, sired five champions. Castle in the Sky has sired seventeen champions to date. His daughter, Ch. Firacres Star Sapphire is a Toy Group winner.

Gloria Lipman (Nikko) of Escondido, California, has bred or owned thirty-five champions including two Best in Show winners, six Group winners and three Specialty winners.

Her imported Ch. Quarnhill Fusspot (Eng. Ch. Murose Storm) sired ten champions. His son, Ch. Nikko's Mr. Independence, was the sire of Best in Show winner, Ch. Nikko's Rolls Royce Corniche.

Ch. Nikko's Here Comes Johnny (Corniche's grandson) is also a Group and Specialty winner, and has sired four champions by mid 1992. Johnny's son, Ch. Nikko's Anchor Man of Bejaze, owned by Linda Bush is also a Group and Specialty winner.

Top of The Line in Hampton Falls, New Hampshire, belongs to Eddy and Linda Nicholson and was the home of two Best in Show winners five Group and two Specialty winners.

Ch. Nikko's Rolls Royce Corniche (a grandson of Ch. Quarnhill Fusspot) won five Bests in Show, thirty-three Groups and sired ten

Ch. Quarnhill Fusspot was imported from England and is owned by
Gloria Lipman for her Nikko Kennels.

Ch. Nikko's Here Comes Johnny, owned and bred by Stanley and
Gloria Lipman. *Missy Yuhl*

Ch. Nikko's Rolls Royce Corniche, bred by the Lipmans and owned by Eddy and Linda Nicholson. *John L. Ashbey*

Ch. Nikko's Silver Cloud, owned by Eddy and Linda Nicholson and bred by the Lipmans, is a daughter of Corniche and, like her sire, she boasts a number of impressive wins.

champions. Corniche's daughter, Ch. Nikko's Silver Cloud, won one Best in Show, seven Groups and a Specialty. Corniche also sired Toy Group winners Ch. Top of the Line Opportunity and Ch. Top of the Line Stock Option.

Top of the Line's Ch. Carousel's Show Biz Kid (Ch. Wildweir Bumper Sticker) won three Groups and one Specialty.

Heskethane, owned by Beryl Hesketh, is located in Wurtsboro, New York, but was started in England, then removed to Venezuela before settling in the United States in 1960.

Ch. Heskethane Blue Tempo sired seventeen champions. His son, Ch. Heskethane Lady's Benjamin, sired nine champions. Benjamin's son, Ch. Heskethane Blue Gem sired five champions.

Tempo's daughter, Ch. Heskethane Blue Honoria, produced six champions as did Honoria's dam Heskethane Wee Countess. Tempo's son Heskethane Jazzbo sired five champions including Carnaby Yorkshires' Ch. Carnaby Rock N' Roll who was an all-breed Best in Show and Specialty winner and sire of eighteen champions.

June and Gene Gorrondona of Kenner, Louisiana, own Ch. Jugene Popeye the Sailor (Ch. Heskethane Lord of Tintagel—a son of Lady's Benjamin) who has sired five champions, including their Group-winning Ch. Jugene's Winning Colours.

Wildweir was started in 1949 in Glenview, Illinois, by Janet E. Bennett and Joan B. Gordon. Miss Bennett passed away in 1985 and in 1986 the kennel name was registered in joint ownership of Joan B. Gordon and Nancy C. Donovan. Nancy has been a part of Wildweir since purchasing her first Yorkie, Ch. Wildweir War Bonnet in 1960.

By mid 1992, Wildweir had owned or bred 237 champions including sixteen Best in Show winners, forty Group winners and thirteen Specialty winners.

The English import, Ch. Little Sir Model (Eng. Ch. Ben's Blue Pride) was purchased in 1950 and became the first Yorkshire to record a Best in Show. He won four Bests and thirty-one groups. His daughter Cover Girl (ex Gayway's Tim's Mite) was the dam of five champions.

Ch. Golden Fame imported in 1951 sired Eng. Ch. Blue Symon and Wildweir Periwinkle and through these two offspring he appears in the background of more Best in Show winners and top producers than any other founding sire. Fame won the breed at the first YTCA match in 1952.

Of all the Wildweir sires the one which most influenced the breed through his descendents was the Irish import Ch. Star Twilight of Clu-

Ch. Little Sir Model, a memorable English import, was the first of the breed to win an all-breed BIS in the United States. He was brought to this country and was owned by Janet E. Bennett and Joan B. Gordon.

Ch. Golden Fame, imported from England and owned by Janet E. Bennett and Joan B. Gordon.   *Frasie Studio*

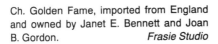

Ch. Star Twilight of Clu-Mor, owned by Janet E. Bennett and Joan B. Gordon, was one of the breed's most outstanding winners and producers. His record included First in the Toy Group at Westminster in 1954 and 1955. To date, he is the only Yorkshire to have won more than one Westminster Group.

Mor (by Eng. & Ir. Ch. Twinkle Star of Clu-Mor) imported in 1950. Star Twilight won twenty-six Bests in Show, eighty-one Groups and five Specialties and sired fifteen champions. He was the breed's record holder until his great-great-grandson, Ch. Cede Higgens took over the record in 1978. His children include Group winner Ch. Wildweir Shining Star (Cover Girl's daughter); Wildweir Beloved Belinda, dam of four champions and Ch. Wildweir Cock of the Walk, sire of five champions. The first bitch to win a Best in Show was Ch. Proud Girl of Clu-Mor (whose dam Clu-Mor Queen of Hearts was Star Twilight's full sister.)

Ch. Prince Moon of Clu-Mor and Ch. Starial of Clu-Mor, imported in 1956, have both played a major role in Wildweir breeding.

Prince Moon was the sire of Ch. Wildweir Ticket to the Moon (a Sorreldene Salome's granddaughter) who was the dam of four champions. Ticket's son, Ch. Wildweir Brass Hat sired ten champions; her daughter Wildweir Hot Fudge produced four champions. Wildweir Time and Tide (Ticket's litter sister) was the dam of nine champions, including Helen and Merrill Cohen's Best in Show winner Ch. Wildweir Prim N' Proper (by Ch. Wildweir Pomp N' Circumstance).

Prince Moon bred to Starial's daughter Ch. Rose Petal of Clu-Mor produced Ch. Wildweir Moonrose who was a Best in Show and Specialty winner and Moonrose's daughter, Ch. Wildweir Belle of the Ball, was a Group winner.

Wildweir Scarlet Ribbon, Ticket To the Moon's daughter, was the dam of ten champions.

Eng. & Am. Ch. Buranthea's Doutelle (Eng. & Ir. Ch. Mr. Pim of Johnstounburn) was imported in 1959. Doutelle was a Best in Show and Specialty winner in England, and in the United States, he won four Bests in Show, twenty-four Groups and two Specialties. He sired ten champions.

Irish import Ir. & Am. Ch. Continuation of Gleno imported in 1968 was a Best in Show and Specialty winner in Ireland and Great Britain. In the United States he won five Bests in Show, twenty-eight Toy Groups, and two Specialties. His daughter, Ch. Wildweir Contrail won three Bests in Show, thirteen Groups and one Specialty. Contrail's son Ch. Wildweir Counterpart won a Best in Show and three Groups.

Of all the dogs bred by Wildweir, the individual that had the most profound influence on the breed would have been Star Twilight's double grandson, Ch. Wildweir Pomp N' Circumstance (Ch. Wildweir Cock of the Walk ex Capri Venus). He sired ninety-five champions

Ch. Wildweir Pomp N' Circumstance, owned and bred by Janet E. Bennett and Joan B. Gordon, is the all-time top-producing sire in the history of the breed with an amazing tally of 95 champion offspring.

Ch. Wildweir Fair N' Square, a son of Pomp N' Circumstance, owned and bred by Janet E. Bennett and Joan B. Gordon, was a noteworthy winner and producer in his own right.

Evelyn Shafer

Ch. Wildweir Respected Legend, a grandson of Fair N' Square, was bred by Nancy Donovan and owned by Zee Daricek.

including three Best in Show winners, and thirteen Toy Group winners. He appears in the background of two thirds of all Best in Show Yorkshire Terriers. The Pomp N' Circumstance son Ch. Wildweir Darktown Strutter, was a Group winner and sired twelve champions including the Naegeles' Ch. Northshire's Mazeltov, sire of thirty-three champions, the Karns' Ch. Darshire Corrigan, sire of nine champions and the Berrys' Ch. Wildweir Doodletown Piper sire of five champions.

Pomp N'Circumstance's son Ch. Wildweir Fair N'Square won three Bests in Show, twenty-five Toy Groups, two Specialties and sired eighteen champions.

Fair N'Square's daughter, Ch. Wildweir Face Card was a Specialty winner. His sons Ch. Wildweir Ham Salad sired five champions and Ch. Cloverwee Magic Marker sired seven champions. Marker's son Wildweir Magic Potion sired six while another Marker son, Ch. Ladylair Moonlight Magic, sired Lordean's top producer, Lordean's Moonlight Lady.

Fair N'Square was the grandsire of Ch. Trivar's Cookie Monster, Ch. Wildweir Bumper Sticker, Specialty winner Ch. Wildweir Respected Legend, sire of seven champions and Ch. Cupoluv's Fair Le Grand, sire of seven champions. The last two are both owned by Zee Daricek (Cupoluv), Avondale, Pennsylvania.

Ch. Wildweir Prim N' Proper (Pomp N' Circumstance ex Wildweir Time And Circumstance) won a Best in Show and sixteen Groups while her son, Ch. Wildweir Briefcase, was a Specialty winner. They were both owned by Helen and Merrill Cohen, Baltimore, Maryland, Briefcase was bred by the Cohens.

Pomp N' Circumstance's daughter, Ruth Cooper's Ch. Wildweir Skater's Waltz, won six Groups and produced five champions. Her brother, Ch. Wildweir Stuffed Shirt sired Francis Cohen's Ch. Wildweir Sandwich Man who won two Best in Shows and sixteen Groups. Stuffed Shirt's son Kirnel's Ch. Wildweir Dinner Jacket sired thirteen champions. Pomp N' Circumstance's son, Tanglewood Eden bred to Fair N'Square's daughter, Wildweir Dowager Duchess produced Ch. Wildweir The Arrogant Duke who sired six champions. Duke's daughters, Ch. Wildweir Doorprize and Ch. Wildweir Wicked Countess, were both Group winners and his son, Ch. Wildweir Duke's Credit, was a Specialty winner. Duke is the grandsire of Ch. Estugo's Dinkel Duke.

Pomp N' Circumstance's son Maybelle Neuguth's Ch. Wildweir

Ch. Wildweir Bumper Sticker, a BIS-winning grandson of Fair N' Square, bred by Janet E. Bennett and Joan B. Gordon. *Martin Booth*

Irish Ch. Gleno Credit Card, imported and owned by Janet E. Bennett and Joan B. Gordon. *Martin Booth*

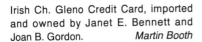

Ch. Wildweir Duke's Credit is a grandson of Credit Card and a Specialty winner. He was bred by Dave and Carol Hilken and owned by Joan Gordon and Nancy Donovan. *Booth photo*

E Major sired ten champions. Major's daughter Fred Wolpert's Ch. Frojo's Blue Button of Maybelle, dam of four champions.

Wildweir's Ch. Doodletown Counterpoint (Ch. Wildweir Doodletown Piper ex Wildweir Forget-Me-Not, dam of four champions) was bred by Vic and Lorraine Berry owners of Doodletown Yorkshires in Newport Beach, California. Counterpoint sired two Best in Show winners and was the grandsire of another. He was the winner of ten Groups and one Specialty.

Counterpoint's son, Ch. Wildweir Bumper Sticker (ex Fair N'Square's daughter, Wildweir Date-line) won twelve Bests in Show, sixty-two Toy Groups and sired eleven champions.

Bumper's son Ch. Wynsippi's Undercover Lover sired five champions. He is the grandsire of Kathleen Kolbert's and Richard Lawrence's German Ch. Turyanne Shannon of Shamrock, sire of nine champions, and Wildweir's Group winner Ch. Northshire Racing Silks.

Counterpoint sired the Best in Show winner, Ch. Wildweir Counterpart. His grandson, Wildweir's Ch. Doodletown Tom Tom, bred by Vic and Lorraine Berry, won a Best in Show and seven Groups and has sired seven champions.

In 1979, Ir. Ch. Gleno Credit Card (Ir. & Eng. Ch. Blairsville Royal Seal) joined Wildweir. He sired seven champions including Lila Kleper's Specialty winner Ch. Leimont's Monty's First Solo. Credit Card's sons Ch. Wildweir Tabaaho has sired five champions and Betty Dullinger's Ch. Wildweir Master Card sired German Ch. Turyanne Shannon of Shamrock.

Kirnel Yorkshires, owned by Nell and Kirill Fietinghoff, of Downey, California, commenced activity in 1953. Ten years later Ch. Kirnel Yum Yum was the first Yorkshire Terrier bitch to win a Specialty.

Kirnel's Ch. Wildweir Coat of Arms (Ch. Buranthea's Doutelle) sired ten champions including Margery May's Ch. Kirnel Topaz Medallion who sired seven champions. Kirnel's Ch. Wildweir Dinner Jacket sired thirteen champions including the Specialty winner, Ch. Kirnel's Buckaroo.

Jean Kasten owns Designer Yorkshires in Chatsworth, California. Her Buckaroo son, Ch. Designer's Doubloon, sired seven champions and Buckaroo's grandson, Ch. Designer's Diamond Dust, sired eight champions.

Am., Mex., Can. Ch. Wildweir Keepsake, a Pomp N' Circumstance son was bred by Janet E. Bennett and Joan B. Gordon and owned by Anne Goldman.

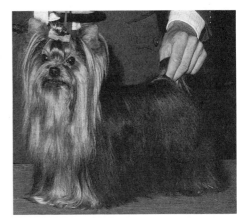

Ch. Kajimanor Olde Spice, bred by Kay Radcliffe and owned by Harry and Chiquita Hansen.

Earl Graham

Ch. Shadomountin Sparrow Hawk, a son of Olde Spice, bred and owned by Kathy Bucher, was Best of Breed at Westminster, 1980 under Janet E. Bennett.   *John L. Ashbey*

Ch. Shadomountin Steppin' Up, a son of Sparrow Hawk, was bred by Kathy Bucher and owned by Janet Jackson.   *Pegini*

Anne Goldman's Starfire prefix started in 1960 in Santa Monica, California. Her Am. & Mex. Ch. Wildweir Keepsake (Ch. Wildweir Pomp N' Circumstance) sired thirty-one champions. His son, Ch. Starfire Mitey Model, sired six champions and Ch. Blue Creek Major Moppet sired five champions. Keepsake was the grandsire of Lee and Richard Sakal's Best in Show winner Ch. Camelot's Little Pixie and Ch. Vi-Clar's Heesa Dandy sire of six champions.

The Topaz prefix was owned by Margery May. Her Ch. Kirnel's Topaz Medallion sired seven champions and his daughter, Ch. Topaz Tertia produced four champions. Topaz's Ch. Starfire Mitey Model sired six champions, and was a Best in Show winner in Canada and a Group winner in the United States. His daughter, Ch. Topaz Vikki's Verity, produced four champions, as did Verity's dam BeeGee's Sue's Victory.

Ka-jo was owned by Carol Fēncl of Wheaton, Illinois, and was established in 1960. Am. & Can. Ch. Ka-jo's Wendy on the Go (Ch. Wildweir Pomp N' Circumstance) was a Group winner. Her son, Ch. Ka-jo's Candyman, was a Group winner and sire of Ch. Ka-jo's Sassafras who had one Best in Show and nine Toy Groups.

Kay Radcliffe's Kajimanor Kennels were located in Rockford, Illinois, and started in 1963. Kajimanor was the home of twenty-two champions. Her Amer. Mex. Can. & Bda. Ch. Wildweir Ten O'Clock Scholar (Ch. Wildweir Pomp N' Circumstance ex Wildweir Dilly-Dally—dam of four champions), won five Groups and sired twenty champions. Scholar's daughters Kajimanor Gay Gypsy and Tykil Trade Secret both produced four champions. His son Ch. Kajimanor Olde Blue sired five champions.

Harry and Chiquita Hansen of Norman, Oklahoma, own Bluecreek Kennels. Their Ch. Kajimanor Olde Spice, a son of Olde Blue, sired twenty-five champions. Their Olde Spice son, Ch. Blue Creek Chili Pepper, sired six champions, and his son Wanda Murphy's Ch. Castle's Song Sung Blue sired five champions. The Olde Spice daughter, Ch. Jen's Chiquita was a Group and Specialty winner.

Kathy Bucher's Shadomountin was located in Claremore Oklahoma. Her Ch. Shadomountin Sparrow Hawk, a son of Ch. Kajimanor Olde Spice, won two Bests in Show, five Groups, a Specialty and was the sire of twenty-five champions. Hawk's sister, Ch. Shadomountin Lucky Penny was a Group winner.

Janet Jackson's Steppin' Up Kennel is located in Duncan, Oklahoma. Her Sparrow Hawk son, Ch. Shadomountin Steppin' Up, has won a Best in Show, seven Groups, two Specialties and has sired nine champions. Her Ch. Shadomountin Upper Cut, Steppin' Up's son, has won four Groups and two Specialties.

Sparrow Hawk's double grandson La Donna Reno's Ch. Shadomountin Whistle Stop has sired five champions.

The Northshire-Yorkies belong to Dorothy and Walter Naegele who started in 1963. They are now located in Berthoud, Colorado. The Naegeles have owned or bred over fifty champions. Their Pomp N' Circumstance daughter Ch. Wildweir Patty of Northshire won three Groups. Amer., Can., Mex., Bda. Ch. Northshire's Mazeltov, a son of Ch. Wildweir Darktown Strutter won ten Groups, a Specialty and sired thirty-four champions. Mazeltov's son, Ferdinand Rent's Ch. Gaitmoor Little Big Man won nine Groups and sired twelve champions including Arlene Johnson's Ch. Pegmate Man About Town who won six Groups and sired six champions. Mazeltov's son, Ch. Northshire's Keyn Hora, also sired six champions, his brother Exmoor's Ch. Northshire Dapper Dan sired eleven champions.

Nancy Hinner's littermate offspring of Mazeltov, Ch. Northshire St. Nick and Ch. Northshire's First Noel each had five champion offspring.

Anderleigh is owned by Barbara Alexander and located in Dublin, Ohio. Her Mazeltov son, Ch. Popan's Chairman of the Board, sired five champions including the brothers, Ch. Anderleigh Junior Executive, sire of five champions, and Ch. Anderleigh Golden Bear, sire of eleven champions. Golden Bear's son, Ch. Jacolyn Tug of War sired nine champions.

The Naegeles' Specialty winner, Ch. Northshire's Dangerous Dan, has sired six champions. His son, Ch. Windwood Meet Mr. Callahan is owned by Sandy Aroch of Elwood, Illinois. Callahan is a Toy Group winner and sire of three champions to date.

Melodylane, of Centerville, Iowa, owned by Mary and Freeman Purvis is the home of Mazeltov's son, Ch. Melodylane Mini Trail. Mini Trail's dam, Melodylane Patti Marie, is the dam of five champions. Mini Trail, himself won nine groups, a Specialty and sired twenty-two champions, including Ch. Melody Lane Right On Man, winner of three Groups, and his sister Janice Zombola's Group winner, Ch. Melodylane's Pink Champagne. The dam of both of these was Melodylane Peppermint Candy who was the dam of seven champions. Champagne, bred to Ch. Clarkwyn Jubilee Eagle, produced the Best in Show winner Ch. Talk of the Town.

Am., Can., Mex. and Berm. Ch. Northshire's Mazel-tov, bred and owned by Walter and Dorothy Naegele, is yet another successful grandson of Pomp N' Circumstance.

Ch. Northshire's Dangerous Dan, a grandson of Bumper Sticker, bred and owned by Walter and Dorothy Naegele. *Phoebe*

Ch. Windwood Meet Mr. Callahan (Ch. North-shire's Dangerous Dan ex Ch. Windwood Mi Amor), bred and owned by Sandra Aroch.
Booth photo

Ch. Carlen's Johnny Walker, bred and owned by Helen Stern.

Ch. Streamglen Luna Star, an English import, owned by Beverly Ferguson and Catherine Sheridan.

Int., Am. Ch. Estugo's Star Gazer, a son of Luna Star, owned by Hugo Ibanez and Steve Maggard.

Ch. Estugo's Dinkel Duke, a son of Stargazer, bred and owned by Hugo Ibanez and Steve Maggard.
Alverson

Helen Stern owns Carlen Yorkshires in Brooklyn, New York. She has been breeding since 1960 when her daughter presented her with a tiny puppy who grew up to be Ch. Kanga's Stinger of Carlen. Mrs. Stern has bred or owned twenty-seven champions to date. Her Ch. Carlen's Johnny Walker, a son of Ch. Cupoluv's Fair Le Grand won a Best in Show, seven Groups, five Specialties and sired six champions. Johnny's daughter Ch. Carlen's Tia Maria is the dam of four champions.

Beverly Ferguson and Catherine Sheridan own Tiffany Kennels in Pasadena, Maryland and they have owned over thirty champions. Their English import, Ch. Streamglen Luna Star, sired eight champions, and one daughter was a Group winner.

Hugo Ibanez and Steve Maggard's Estugo Yorkshires started in 1976 in Charlotte, New Carolina, and the partners have owned thirty-six champions. Their son of Luna Star, Ch. Estugo's Stargazer won four Groups and sired eight champions. Stargazer's son, Ch. Estugo's Dinkel Duke has sired five champions to date and is the sire of Ch. Estugo's Bill Dollar. Estugo's Ch. Wynsippi's Under Cover Lover sired by Ch. Wildweir Bumper Sticker sired five champions.

Wynsippi was owned by Virginia Knoche in Warsaw, Illinois. Ch. Wynsippi's Dusty Dawn sired six champions, and Mrs. Knoche bred Turyanne's Group winner Ch. Wynsippi's Mr. Dinks. Sheri and Willowe Linde's Best in Show and Specialty winner, Ch. Genie's Lil' Duke, was sired by Ch. Genie's Sinbad of Wynsippi out of Wynsippi Sanron Jenny Lynn.

Dusty Dawn's brother, Ch. Zerox Sirrocco, of Wynsippi is owned by T. Conner who uses the Zerox prefix and is located in La Mesa, California. He also owns Ch. Zerox the Midas Touch, sire of ten champions including Joyce Watkin's Best in Show winner, Ch. Marcris A Touch of Midas, who has sired five champions. Midas Touch is the sire Ch. Rothby Rex at Marcliff and Ch. Rothby Reflection. Midas' son Ch. Zerox Raisin Cane is a Specialty winner.

Since 1979 Turyanne in Newtown, Connecticut, has been owned by Kathleen Kolbert and Richard Lawrence. However Kathleen has been a breeder since 1963, breeding under the kennel name Windsor, and then Windsor-Gayelyn with Marilyn Koenig for nine years. Turyanne is a continuation of these lines with the addition of imported dogs based on the Millmoor line from Belgium. In all, Turyanne has owned or bred over ninety champions.

Ch. Ozmilion Play Boy (Eng. Ch. Heavenly Blue of Wiske) was

imported from England in 1971 and sired five champions. Turyanne's Ch. Wynsippi's Mr. Dinks won three Toy Groups and a Specialty. Ch. Windsor-Gayelyn Robin was a Group winner. Ch. Turyanne's Pandora Box won a Specialty and the imported International and American Ch. Uddersfiel Ben de Penghibur has won two Groups.

German Ch. Turyanne Shannon of Shamrock (Ch. Wildweir Master Card ex Ch. Leprechaun's Bumper Shoot) was successfully shown and used at stud in Europe. He sired nine champions (two American and seven foreign) including Millmoor's World Ch. My Precious Keep Up.

Morris Howard and Johnny Robinson started their Trivar line in 1960 in Potomac, Maryland. They have bred or owned over 110 champions which include seven Bests in Show, nine Group and seven Specialty winners.

Ch. Dandy Diamond of Mayfair sired Ch. Trivar's Bon Vivant who sired five champions. One of these was the Best in Show winner, Victor Recond, and Jerry Vine's Ch. Trivar's Princess Jervic.

Bon Vivant, bred to Trivar's Contessa the dam of ten champions, produced Ch. Trivar's Tycoon, winner of a Best in Show, thirty-one Toy Groups and a Specialty and the sire of fifty-four champions. Tycoon's brother, Ch. Trivar's Arslan Trailblazer sired Paul Thomas' Best in Show and Specialty winner, Ch. Arslan Darwin Darby.

Contessa's daughter Ch. Trivar's Country Girl was the dam of four champions. Country Girl's sire was Ch. Yorksmith Fosdick of Mayfair who sired seven champions.

Ch. Trivar's Gold Digger, Tycoon's daughter (ex May Queen of Astolat who was the dam of four champions), won two Bests in Show and thirteen Groups. Tycoon's son Ch. Trivar's Suds Sipper won nineteen Bests in Show, sixty-four groups and two Specialties. Ch. Trivar's Cookie Monster, Tycoon's son and a grandson of Ch. Wildweir Fair N'Square, won ten Bests in Show, forty-two Groups, two Specialties and sired forty-nine champions to date.

Cookie's son, Ch. Trivar's Diddly Squat won four Bests in Show, thirty-eight Groups, a Specialty and sired five champions. Cookie bred to Ch. Trivar's Hell's Angel, a Tycoon daughter and the dam of seven champions, produced Group and Specialty winner Ch. Trivar's Bit 'R Sweet Briar owned by Dianna M. Wright of Pomfret, Maryland.

Ch. Trivar's Holiday Spirit produced four champions and her daughter Ch. Trivar's Peppermint Patty was the dam of five champions.

German Ch. Turyanne Shannon of Shamrock, a grandson of Bumper Sticker and Credit Card, owned by Kathleen Kolbert.

Ch. Trivar's Tycoon, bred and owned by Johnny Robinson and Morris Howard.

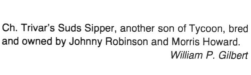

Ch. Trivar's Cookie Monster, a son of Tycoon, bred and owned by Johnny Robinson and Morris Howard.

Ch. Trivar's Suds Sipper, another son of Tycoon, bred and owned by Johnny Robinson and Morris Howard.
William P. Gilbert

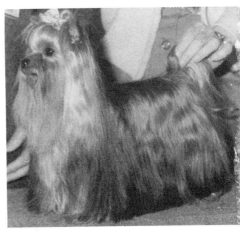

Ch. Toy Clown of Rusklyn, imported by Wildweir Kennels and owned by Ila Clark.

Ch. Clarkwyn Jubilee Eagle, a grandson of Ch. Toy Clown, bred by Ila Clark and owned by Ruth Jenkins.

Ch. Wenscoe's Whizzaway of Tzumiao, imported from England by Wendy Anne Whiteley and owned by Ruth Jenkins.

Ch. Finstal Royal Icing, another English import owned by Ruth Jenkins.

Ch. Trivar's Sugar Dumpling produced six champions while Ch. Trivar's Taffy and Trivar's Bonnie each produced four champions.

Clarkwyn, owned by Ila Clark, started in 1958 in Seattle Washington. Her Ch. Toy Clown of Rusklyn was imported by Wildweir and purchased by Mrs. Clark in 1960. He won ten Toy Groups and sired five champions.

Her foundation bitch, Clarkwyn Debutante, Pretoria Action's granddaughter bred to Ch. Wildweir Pomp N' Circumstance produced Ch. Clarkwyn Dreamy Doll, the dam of Ch. Clarkwyn Nipsey Doodle. Doodle bred to Toy Clown's daughter, Ch. Clarkwyn Fanciful Sue, produced four champions including Ruth Jenkins' Ch. Clarkwyn Jubilee Eagle, Ann Hayden's Ch. Clarkwyn Jamboree Eagle and Frank and Agnes Hattori's Group and Specialty winner Ch. Clarkwyn Double Eagle who sired five champions. Toy Clown's daughter Clarkwyn's Flirtation was the dam of Mr. and Mrs. Charles Mansfield's Best in Show and Specialty winner Ch. Heart G's Spunky Sparky. Toy Clown's daughter, Ch. Clarkwyn Gina Marie was the dam of four champions.

Ch. Wenscoe's Whizzaway of Tzumiao was imported by Wendy Anne Whiteley and sired thirteen champions. His daughter Ch. Wenscoe's Whynot of Shaumar was a Best in Show winner, and his son, Ch. Wenscoe's Zipperdee Du Dah, sired five Champions.

Alice Haman owns Beholda Yorkies and her son of Whizzaway Beholda Blueprint has sired eleven champions. Blueprint's son Ch. Beholda Flyaway Jack sired five champions. Jack sired Ch. Beholda Schlemeil, the sire of five champions and Delores Kauffman's Beholda Glow, the dam of seven champions.

Dorothy Guant owns Dot's Yorkies in Covina, California. She has owned over forty-seven champions. Her son of Flyaway Jack, Ch. Dot's Top Banana sired sixteen champions. Her Dot's Bright Light a daughter of Ch. Cede Higgens produced six champions, and Maureen Vandenburg's Ch. Dot's Constant Comment has produced six champions to date.

Ruth Jenkins started Jentre in Issaquah, Washington in 1969 and has owned over fifty-five champions. Both Ch. Wenscoe's Whizzaway of Tzumiao and his son Ch. Wenscoe's Zipperdee Du Dah joined Jentre when Mrs. Whiteley retired from breeding. Whizzaway sired Ch. Juana and Jentre's Blue Jeans who produced ten champions. Blue Jeans' dam, Ch. Jentre's Josephine, Jubilee Eagle's daughter, produced four champions. Blue Jeans' daughters Ch. Jentre's Sheen of Queba was the dam of eight champions and Ch. Jentre's Pastorial Sugar Tyme produced nine champions. Both were sired by Ch. Clarkwyn Jubilee Eagle.

Jentre's top stud Ch. Clarkwyn Jubilee Eagle was a Group winner and sired fifty-two champions. He was the dominant influence in the breed in the 1970s and 1980s. He sired three Best in Show winners; Ch. Cede Higgens, Ch. My Flying Colours at Jentre, and Ch. Cameo Talk of the Town, and Specialty winners Ch. Robtell Jubilation, Ch. Fardust Fury, who sired fourteen champions, and the brothers Ch. Jentre's Beau Gentry and Ch. Jentre's Special Delivery, whose dam Jentre's Am. & Can. Ch. Carmate Sugar Cookie was the dam of eight champions.

English import Ch. Finstal Royal Icing (Eng. Ch. Finstal Jonathon) joined Jentre in 1984 and has sired to date thirty-two champions, and won two Specialties.

Barbee, owned by Bill and Barbara Switzer in Seattle, Washington, began in 1973 when the Switzers purchased the future Ch. Cede Higgens from his breeder C. D. Lawrence. Handled by the Switzers' daughter Marlene Lutovsky he became the all-time top winner in the breed and the only Yorkie to win Best in Show at Westminster. His win at Westminister in 1978 signaled his retirement from competition or his record might have been even larger.

Barbee has bred or owned four Best in show winners, nine Group winners, seven Specialty winners and over fifty-five champions. Ch. Cede Higgens won thirty-three Bests in Show, seventy-one Groups, ten specialties and sired thirty-four champions. Higgens' son Ch. Robtell Sting won a Best in Show, twenty Toy Groups and a Specialty.

Higgens' son Ch. Barbee Denaire Dickens won three Groups and Joan Yost's Ch. Barbee Notorius won a Best in Show, twenty-seven Groups and has sired five champions.

Ch. Barbee Goodtime Charlie, another Higgens son won two Bests in Show, eleven Groups, two Specialties and sired ten champions including Ch. Lordean The Angel Maker. The Higgens son, Ch. Barbee Double-O-Seven, sired eleven champions including Group winner Ch. Barbee You'll Love It and Specialty and Group winner, Ch. Barbee I'm Bad, both owned by Dr. Larry and Jeanine Snyder. Ch. Barbee My Cup of Tea, a Higgens daughter is also a Group and Specialty winner.

Lori Williams started Lordean in Kuna, Idaho, in 1979. Her Ch.

THE STUFF DREAMS ARE MADE OF—Best in Show at Westminster is one of the dog sport's most coveted honors and has come but once to a Yorkshire Terrier. The dog was Ch. Cede Higgens, owned by Bill and Barbara Switzer and bred by C.D. Lawrence. The year was 1978 and the judge was the highly respected Anne Rogers Clark. Higgens was piloted to this win of a lifetime by his owners' daughter, Marlene Lutovsky. *William P. Gilbert*

Ch. Barbee's Good Time Charlie, a BIS Higgens son, owned and bred by Bill and Barbara Switzer. *Carl Lindemaier*

Ch. Barbee I'm Bad, a grandson of Ch. Cede Higgens, bred by the Switzers and owned by Dr. Larry and Jeanine Snyder. *Nathan Ham*

Jusbecus Blue Creek Muffin, a Ch. Blue Creek Chili Pepper daughter, was the dam of seven champions. Bred to Ch. Barbee Goodtime Charlie, Muffin produced Ch. Lordean The Angel Maker, sire of eighteen champions.

Angel Maker bred to Ch. Eden Valley Crystal Blue, the dam of seven champions, produced Ch. Lordean's Teen Angel who won three Toy Groups and sired six champions. His son, Ch. Lordean's Patent Bear sired thirteen champions to date. Among his sons, Sue Sorenson's Ch. Lordean's Magic Maker has a Best in Show, four Groups and three Specialties and Lezle Treadwell's Ch. Lordean's The Silk Showman is a Group and Specialty winner.

Lordean's Moonlight Magic is the dam of ten champions to date.

Martell Roberts owns Robtell Yorkshires in Bonney Lake, Washington. Her Am. & Can. Ch. Robtell Jubilation, a son of Jubilee Eagle, won sixteen Groups, three Specialties and sired nine champions.

Mistangay was owned by Renee Emmons in Atlantic City, New Jersey. After her death in 1989, the kennel has been carried on by her husband Al Emmons. Her Ch. Jentre's Charger of Mistangay (a son of Jubilee Eagle ex Jentre's Robina, a daughter of Ch. Wenscoe's Zipperdee Du Dah) is the sire of thirty-one champions. His offspring have been very influential in the breed in the 1980s and early 1990s. The Charger son, Ch. Mistangay Angelo has sired twelve champions.

Angelo's daughter Ch. Denaire Mistangay Malissa produced six champions. Malissa's dam, Ch. Denaire Dawn at Mistangay, a Ch. Finstal Royal Icing daughter, was the dam of eleven champions. Dawn's dam Ch. Denaire Fame, a granddaughter of Ch. Mayfair-Barban Quinnat, was a Group winner and dam of nine champions.

Malissa's full brother, Ch. Mistangay Gilbey has won a Best in Show, fifteen Toy Groups, four Specialties and has sired six champions.

Rose Anne Hayes' Ch. Farkee's Desi of Abbeydale, a Charger son, sired seven champions. Susan Griffin of Dallas, Texas, owns the Peppertree prefix and her Desi son, Ch. Peppertree Montage, is a Group and Specialty winner. Montage's dam, Ch. Peppertree Collage, a daughter of Ch. Castle's Song Sung Blue, is the dam to date of seven champions.

Roberta Rothenbach, owner of Rothby Yorkshires in Elgin, Illinois, has been breeding since 1967. Her Ch. Rothby Rex at Marcliff won five Groups and sired twenty champions. Rex's sister, Ch. Rothby Reflection is the dam of five champions and is herself a Group winner.

Am., Can. Ch. Lordean's Teen Angel, a grandson of Ch. Barbee's Good Time Charlie, was bred and owned by Lori Williams. *Carl Lindemaier*

Am., Can. Ch. Lordean's Magic Maker, bred by Lori Williams and owned by Sue Sorenson, is an all-breed BIS and Specialty winner. *Meg Callea*

Am., Can. Ch. Robtel Jubilation, a son of Ch. Clarkwyn Jubilee Eagle, owned and bred by Martell Roberts.

Ch. Mistangay Gilbey, bred by Renee Emmons and owned by Alfred Emmons. *John L. Ashbey*

Ch. Rothby's Reneegade, a son of Ch. Jentre's Charger of Mistangay, bred, owned and handled by Roberta Rothenbach.

K. Booth

Ch. Rothby Rex at Marcliff, shown here at seven years when he won the Veterans' class at the 1986 Greater New York Specialty under Jane Forsyth. He was owned and handled by Roberta Rothenbach.   *DiGiacomo*

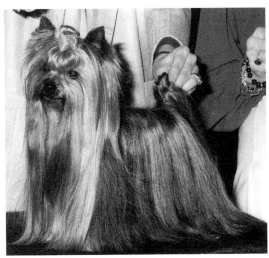

Ch. Rothby's Rambo of Yorktowne, bred by Roberta Rothenbach and owned by Michael and Ethel Fiegelson. A multiple BIS and Specialty winner, Rambo has been handled by Mr. Fiegelson to his impressive record of wins.

L. Sosa

Ch. Mistangay Boom Boom Mancini, a Charger grandson, was bred by Renee Emmons and owned by Ron and Barbara Scott.

Ch. Stratford's Magic, another Charger grandson, was bred and is owned by Ron and Barbara Scott. Magic is a multiple BIS and Specialty winner.

Ch. Denaire Royal Lace, a son of Ch. Finstal Royal Icing, was bred by Paul Katzakian and owned by Ron and Barbara Scott.   *Stephen Klein*

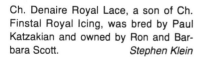

Ch. Caraneal's Charged and Ready, owned and bred by Robert and Georgette Franzoni, was BB at the Yorkshire Terrier Club of America's 1991 winter Specialty under British authority Brian Lister. Mrs. Franzoni handled the dog to this outstanding win. *DiGiacomo*

Ch. Caraneal's Targa, a son of Charger, bred and owned by Robert and Georgette Franzoni.

Rex's son, Natlee Robert's Ch. Natlee's Howard Huge, has a Best in Show and eight Toy Groups.

Reflection bred to Ch. Jentre's Charger of Mistangay produced Rothby's top winner and top sire Ch. Rothby Reneegade. This dog has two Bests in Show, seven Groups, four Specialties and to date has sired forty-seven champions.

Reneegade's son, Ch. Rothby Rennaisance, was a Group winner in the United States and won Best in Show in Taiwan. Reneegade's daughter, Ch. Rothby's Diamond-T Darci and his son Ch. Bluebell's Valentino are both Specialty winners.

Both Ch. Rothby's Royal Rendition and Zerox Ms. Rothby have five champion offspring. Rambo's sister, Rothby's Riff Raff also produced five champions.

Michael and Ethel Fiegelson own Yorktowne kennels in Birmingham, Alabama. Their Ch. Rothby's Rambo of Yorktowne, a son of Zerox Ms. Rothby and Marshona Star Trek, won three Bests in Show, twenty-three Toy Groups, a Specialty and sired eight champions. Rambo's daughter Ch. Yorkboro Great Balls Of Fire (ex Ch. Yorkboro All-Time High) is a Group winner.

Jim Hupp and Bret Walker own Exmoor Yorkshires in Kokomo, Indiana. Their Ch. Jofre's Regal Eagle of Exmoor, a son of Ch. Clarkwyn Double Eagle, won a Best in Show and eight Groups and sired seven champions. Regal Eagle's granddaughter and Reneegade's daughter Ch. Exmoor's One Better has a Best in Show, twenty-two Groups and three Specialties to date.

Stratford is owned by Ron and Barbara Scott in Mechanicsburg, Pennsylvania. Their Ch. Mistangay Boom Boom Mancini, a son of Ch. Mistangay Angelo and Ch. Denaire Dawn at Mistangay has won two Specialties and five Groups. Their Ch. Stratford Magic is also an Angelo son. He is a Best in Show, winner with numerous Groups and two Specialties. Magic's dam, Ch. Denaire Royal Lace, a full sister of Ch. Denaire Dawn at Mistangay is the dam to date of seven champions.

Robert and Georgette Franzoni own Caraneal in Warrenton, Virginia. Their Ch. Caraneal's Targa, a son of Charger, has won two Specialties, and their Ch. Caraneal Charged and Ready, another Charger son ex Ch. Robtell Kristi Luv, a daughter of Ch. Robtell Jubilation, has won ten Groups and four Specialties to date, and has sired six champions.

Ch. Jentre's Charger of Mistangay, owned by Renee Emmons and bred by Ruth Jenkins, was sired by Jubilee Eagle and appears in the pedigrees of several noted winners. *Hess*

5

Introduction to the Standard

PRESCRIBED STANDARDS are useful things. They can help us buy clothes to the right fit, measure the ingredients for a cake, and even set values for a monetary system. In purebred dogs, the word "standard" identifies the written and approved concept of the ideal dog of the breed.

Most breeds were originated to serve mankind in some specific way. The Yorkshire Terrier stems from the little rough terriers of Great Britain—little terriers that killed rats around the farmyard and caught small game for the master's table. This little dog worked in water, over hills and dales, and underground to bolt small game. It was small enough to carry in a pouch or saddlebag, and got along on small rations.

By degrees, breeders became interested in not only keeping this ratting ability, but in preserving a specific *type*. A local keeper of a public house, looking for some way to improve his patronage, would provide a place where a gathering of fanciers could show off their specimens—not only in action, but in form. Thus conformation became a consideration, and rules were drawn up. The criterion brought to light desired points, and soon, from this touchstone, the breed had—in a rough way—developed a standard.

However, a hitch has developed too. Through the years, word meanings change. For example, today we speak of people "doing their own thing." But back in the time of the Vikings, a "thing" was a place for an assembly or council.

The Yorkie standard has many words that make true sense only if we take the pains to interpret them as intended by the establishers of the standard. To do this, we must take into account the dog's origin, its use, and the literal meaning of the words. We must keep in mind, too, that the points desired for the breed are tied genetically to other points in the breed. The standard abides as a guard. If we lose the concepts tailored by those who originated the breed's identity, we wind up with dogs that—albeit sound—are lacking in the qualities that distinguish them as Yorkshire Terriers.

Therefore, before going on to today's AKC-approved standard, let's look back at some of the first full Yorkie descriptions on record.

Among the earliest descriptions of show or breed type comes this, in 1872 from *The Dog* by Idestone. In his chapter on "The Broken-Haired Fox Terrier," Idestone writes:

> Manchester has produced a sort of late years called Scotch Terrier, with a long silky forelock covering the face and eyes. These are invariably Blue-grey, Tan or Black-Tan and they are large or toy size. I imagine they are manufactured from those for which Peter Eden was famed. I have seen—I think at Middleton—the stock dog from which most of these dogs come, and the best class I ever saw was produced at that exhibition; for these men in rags refused offers of twenty or thirty guineas from the London dealers, and they were not far wrong, as the breed has become exceedingly fashionable and second-rate specimens— first-rate ones are never in the market—readily fetch twenty or thirty guineas each. A good blue, a rich tan, length and silky texture of forelock, symmetry and clearness of marks, are the great points of excellence, whilst the prevalence of the blue tinge is never passed over, and generally carries the day.
>
> These dogs require constant attention, and are carefully brushed, combed and cultivated, as one lump of felt is soon succeeded by another, and a tangled coat is fatal to all chances of success. Great roguery is committed by the dishonest in the dressing and staining of these dogs, but the chicanery has hitherto never escaped detection as judging takes place in daylight and even heightened color is transparently visible to a practiced judge.

Dogs of this breed are generally cropped, but it does not add to their beauty as the ears are scarcely visible. The coat is profuse on the body, the tail is not very bushy; the feet are short-coated; the eyes rather full; the mustache moderate; the tan is profuse and blended into a black saddle, and the general texture is soft and silky; the back should be silvery, with a mixture of slate or blue; this should prevail on face and legs.

The dog is hard to describe and difficult to judge, requiring a practiced eye, acute observation, and adroit comparison. The oldest dogs are generally the most taking; none are thoroughly coated until they are over two years old, and much allowance must be made for age. They are also called Yorkshire and Lancashire Terriers, and the best I have seen have come from the latter county, with the exception of Mr. Foster's.

Though this is not a standard, we feel it would take more than practice, acuteness and adroitness to sort out. The general picture of a long-coated Toy dog with soft, silky hair of a blue and tan color is taking form. Already the distinct facet of its being is its coat and color.

The next approach to a description of a show Yorkshire Terrier comes from *Dogs: Their Points, Whims, Instinct and Peculiarities,* edited by Henry Webb and published in 1872.

From the pages of this book, voices trail down from the past offering us a description of Crab and Kitty's grandson; a dog that appears in Huddersfield Ben's pedigree as a great-grandparent, a great-great-grandparent and a great-great-great-grandparent. Which should blow to the four winds the voices that offer us the theory that the Yorkie just blew like a falling leaf into the world of dogdom. This type of breeding can only be called controlled inbreeding.

The dog mentioned in Mr. Webb's treatise was Old Sandy who was registered by The Kennel Club as a Yorkshire Terrier, though his great-grandson Huddersfield Ben beat him into the registry.

Mr. Webb says in 1872:

Mr. Spink's Scotch Terriers are well known and we have great pleasure in being able to give photographs of his most celebrated dogs; Old Sandy (commonly called Huddersfield Sandy) was unfortunately stolen on his way home from Brighton in 1866, after winning the first prize at the dog show. His weight was seven pounds, a very rich tan, golden head, deep blue and a very straight, rather strong, hair, but very bright. Illustrated by photo are: Silk, also a prize dog; Doctor; and Punch, who

The photo montage of Mr. Spink's Scotch Terriers is referred to in the accompanying text. These are believed to be the earliest photos of Yorkshire Terrier ancestry known. The numbers identify: "Silk" (47); "Doctor" (46) and "Punch" (48).

has won a large number of prizes. Mr. Spink says that the Scotch Terrier should be bred as follows:

"The head rather long, with hair falling down considerably below the jaw, golden color at the sides and on ears, also on the muzzle and mustachios; hair on the back long and perfectly straight, good rich blue and very bright; legs and feet well tanned and not too much feathered; tail perfectly straight and well carried; shape firm and compact, not too long on the legs, broad chest and tanned; there must be no white on any part of the body, not even the slightest suspicion of curl or wave on the coat, and the hair fine and bright in quality. The blue and tan should contrast so well as to please the eye, rich and decided in color, and not a sickly silver color all over."

Slowly the rules that would model the Yorkshire Terrier were being laid down, rules that make him a distinct member of the family of purebred dogs.

The next informant on the Yorkshire Terrier's points is Hugh Dalziel from Mr. Walsh's book, *Dogs of the British Islands,* published in 1878. His description of their general appearance leaves one feeling that he wasn't too keen on the breed.

He may be described as the newest goods of this class from the Yorkshire loom; with the greater propriety that his distinctive character is in his coat—well carded, soft and long as it is and beautifully tinted with 'cunning Huddersfield dyes' and free from even a suspicion of 'shoddy.'

Visitors to our dog shows, who look out for the beautiful as well as the useful, cannot fail to be attracted by this little exquisite, as he reclines on his cushion of silk or velvet, in the centre of his little palace of crystal and mahogany, or struts round his mansion, with the consequential airs of the dandy that he is; yet with all his self-assertion of dignity, his beard of approved cut and color, faultless whiskers of Dundreary type, and coat of absolute perfection, without one hair awry, one cannot help feeling that he is but a dandy after all, and would look but a poor scarecrow in dishabille and, possibly too, on account of his dwelling, or reception room, in the construction of which art is mostly set at defiance, one is apt to leave him with the scarcely concealed contempt for a Scion of the 'Veneering family' who, in aping the aristocrat, fail as *parvenus* do. Such as he is, however, there can be little doubt that should ever a canine Teufelsdröckh promulgate a philosophy of clothes for the benefit of his species, the Yorkshire Terrier will represent the dandiacal body: Whilst, in striking contrast, those everyday drudges, the Irish Terriers and Scotch Terriers, with their coarse, ragged unkempt coats will be exhibited as the 'bog-trotter' and 'stock-o-duds' sects of the doggy family.

Mr. Ash then quotes Mr. Dalziel as giving the breed's points in 1878:

The head is small, rather flat on the crown, and together with the muzzle, much resembles, in shape, the Skye Terrier. The eyes, only seen when the "fall" or hair of the face is parted, were also small, keen and bright. The ears, when entire, are either erect, with a slight falling over at the tip or quite pricked.

The legs and feet, although scarcely seen, were to be straight and good, or the dog would have a deformed appearance.

The tail is usually docked, and shows abundance of feathering.

The coat long, straight and silky; must not have any appearance of curl or crimping, and, if wavy, it must be very slightly so; but many excellent specimens have the coat slightly waved.

He writes that he does not know the utmost extent to which the coat has been grown, but supposes it to be 10 to 12 inches.

The colour is one of the most essential things to be looked for in the Yorkshire Terrier; so important is it and so fully is this recognized by exhibitors, that it is said some specimens are shown at times not quite innocent of plum bags and things judiciously applied. They are really blue and tan terriers, and the blue ranges from the clear silvery hue of a deep sky-blue and a blue-black. All dogs, I believe, get lighter in color as they age. The tan on the head should be golden, and the "fall," or hair over the face, gets silvery towards the ends; the tan is deeper on the whiskers and about the ears and on the legs.

They vary in size considerably, so much so that I advocate most strongly making two classes for them, for it is utterly absurd to class any of this breed as a broken-haired terrier, as The Kennel Club does, regardless of the plain meaning of the words. What can be more stupid than to give one of these terriers a prize in his own proper class and proper designation, and his own mother a prize in the broken-haired toy class?

He gives the weights and heights of some of the leading dogs:

"Smart" (Mrs. Foster's), age 3 years, weight 10 lbs.; height 12 inches; length from nose to set of tail, 22 inches.

"Sandy" (Mrs. Foster's), age 2 years, weight 4¾ lbs.; height 9 inches; length from nose to set of tail, 19 inches.

Six years run between the two 1872 descriptions and Mr. Dalziel's of 1878. During this period the specification of points desired had increased even to the point of criticism. The Yorkshire Terrier had now

AN INTERESTING REFLECTION OF HUMANE CONCERNS IN VICTORIAN ENG-LAND: These drawings of various Toy Terriers (including the Yorkshire) were the work of Arthur Wardle and were prepared for two different printings of Rawdon Lee's *Modern Dogs*. In the top drawing, done prior to 1895, all the models show cropped ears; the lower version was drawn in 1896 following the ban on ear cropping in Great Britain. The dogs are the same but their difference is obvious.

acquired a criterion for head, eyes, muzzle, ears, legs, tail and size. Yet the emphasis remained on its shining glory—the distinction that places it apart from other canines—its required coat color and silken long coat.

This emphasis can be seen in the Yorkie's description given in 1887, in *The Dogs of Great Britain, America and Other Countries* written by Stonehenge, together with chapters by American writers. It goes:

> As they are always shown in full dress, little more than outline of shape is looked for; the eye, except when the hair is tied up is invisible; the tail is shortened, and the ear is generally cut. When uncut, it must be small and is preferred when it drops slightly at the tip, but this is a trivial point, and sinks into insignificance before coat and color; the coat must be abundant over the whole body, head, legs and tail, and artificial means are used to encourage its growth; length and straightness, freedom from curl and waviness being sought for; the body color should be clear, soft, silvery blue of course varying in shade; with this is preferred a golden tan head, with darker tan about ears, and rich tan legs. The style in which the coat is arranged for exhibition is beautifully shown in the sketch of Katie; but that stage of perfection is not attained without much time, trouble and patience. When the pups are born they are black in color, as are pepper Dandie Dinmonts and others; at an early age, the tip of the tail is nipped off to the desired length, the ears, if cut at all, not until the age of six to eight months, and before this the coat will be changing color, getting gradually lighter. To prevent the hair being scratched and broken, little or no meat is given.

From these beginning sketches, the costuming came into play. By degrees, his general appearance was brought to the fore. Reference was made to body shape and action. Rules were drawn, models fixed and the breed characteristics established. Words set down as descriptions of early show Yorkshire Terriers have descended to us as part of our present Standard.

Hunting for a positive date for the first accepted Yorkshire Terrier Standard leaves one trailing through contradictive testimony. Mr. P. H. Coombs, in a book copyrighted in 1891, includes a standard he says was accepted by the Yorkshire Terrier Club of England in 1890. Mrs. Munday, Mrs. Swan and Colonel Whitehead in their respective books—*The Yorkshire Terrier*—hold with the Standard being accepted by The Yorkshire Terrier Club in 1898, with no mention of the former Club. Other English writers say the first accepted Standard was drawn up by The Y.T.C. in London at a general meeting on January 5, 1911. And littering up the trail further, Mrs. Mallock includes in her American books—published in 1907 and 1925—what she claims to be the Standard.

Mr. P. H. Coombs has this version of the first Standard in *The American Book of the Dogs*, edited by G. O. Shields, copyright 1891 (Yorkie Article by Coombs):

Quantity and color of hair on back	25
Quality of coat	15
Tan	15
Head	10
Eyes	5
Mouth	5
Ears	5
Legs and Feet	5
Body and General Appearance	10
Tail	5
Total	100

General appearance. This should be of a long-coated pet dog, the coat hanging quite straight and evenly down each side, a parting extending from the nose to the end of the tail. The animal should be compact and neat, the carriage being very "sprightly" bearing an important air. Although the frame is hidden beneath a mantle of hair, the general outline should be such as to suggest the existence of a vigorous and well-proportioned body.

Head. This should be rather small and flat, not too prominent or round in skull, rather broad at the muzzle, with a perfectly black nose; the hair on the muzzle very long, which should be a rich deep tan, not sooty or gray. Under the chin, long hair about the same color as the center of the head, which should be a bright golden tan and not on any account intermingled with dark or sooty hairs. Hair on the sides of the head should be very long and a few shades deeper than the center of the head, especially about the ear-roots.

The Eyes should be of medium size, dark in color, having a sharp, intelligent expression, and placed so as to look directly forward but should not be prominent. The edges of the eyelids should be of a darker color.

Ears, cut or uncut. If cut quite erect; uncut, small, V-shaped, and carried semi-erect. Covered with short hair. Color to be a deep, dark tan.

The Mouth should be good and even; teeth as sound as possible. A dog having lost a tooth or two through accident not the least objectionable, providing the jaws are even.

The Body should be very compact with a good loin, and level on top of the back.

Coat. The hair as long and straight as possible (not wavy), which should be flossy, not woolly. It should extend from the back of the head to the root of tail. Color a bright steel-blue, and on no account intermingled with fawn, light or dark hairs.

Legs quite straight, of a bright, golden-tan color, and well covered with hair, a few shades lighter at the ends than at the roots.

Feet as round as possible; toe-nails black.

Weight divided into two classes, viz; under five pounds and over five pounds, but not to exceed twelve pounds.

Referring to the Standard, Mr. Wilkinson says: "Personally, I confess a weakness for color over quantity of coat, as I contend it is quite possible to produce a vast quantity of coat on a specimen otherwise indifferent. From boyhood, I remember my father (now deceased) being a great breeder and fancier of Yorkshire Terriers, and he could not tolerate a dog without the rich golden tan, and I certainly inherit his weakness, and think points most difficult to obtain should be thought most highly of when they are produced. I am rather afraid that, of late years, too much thought has been given to length of coat in preference to good color and moderate coat combined. A lot of hair with a dog attached does not constitute a perfect Yorkshire Terrier."

Mr. Bootman also says with relation to this point: "Richness of tan on head and legs should, to my mind, be more cultivated than at present. This property was highly prized by the old breeders. The craze for length of coat has in great measure been the means of reducing the quality of tan."

In *Toy Dogs* by Lillian C. Raymond-Mallock, published by Dogdom Publishing Co., Battle Creek, Michigan, in 1907, only a few changes appear. She goes on: "Coat, which should be glossy like silk (not woolly)." She also adds: "not intermingled the least with fawn, light, or dark hairs."

Mrs. Mallock then puts a description of the tail into the Standard: "Tail—cut to medium length, with plenty of hair on, darker blue in color than the rest of the body, especially at the end of the tail and carried a little higher than the end of the back."

Luckily there are clues spread around that make it evident what transpired and why; Mr. Coombs and Mrs. Mallock held to a standard that did not conform to the one accepted by The Kennel Club and the American Kennel Club.

In *The Twentieth Century Dog (Non-Sporting)* published in London in 1904, the author, Herbert Compton, sheds a great deal of light with the following excerpts:

> What the Whippet is to the miners of Northumberland—what the Bulldog was reputed to be the horny-handed sons of toil—that place the Yorkshire Terrier fills in the cottages of the weavers and workers in certain manufacturing districts. Although it has been taken up by fanciers of light and leading, and by dames of high degree, it is really a working man's pet, and his ewe-lamb in a way.
>
> And now for a description of the subject of this article. I am happy in having two at my disposal, and as there are differences of opinion in the fancy, I have no hesitation in giving them both.
>
> Mr. F. Randall: "In my opinion the type of Yorkshire Terrier now shown in London and the South cannot be improved. I consider the dark, steel-blue (not silver) a great improvement on the pale-coloured dogs, which seem to generally be preferred in the North, and are easier to breed than the darker ones."
>
> Mr. Fred Poole (representing the North): "I am quite satisfied with type, as I think a good specimen of today is as near perfection as it is possible to get. My club, the Halifax and District Yorkshire Terrier Club, is the oldest society in existence of its kind and going very strong, with plenty of members. All the Champion dogs of the past and present owe their origin to Halifax, such as Halifax Marvel, the sire of these three noted dogs, Ch. Ted, Ch. Merry Mascot and Ch. Ashton Queen."

Then Mr. Compton continues: "The following are the points of the Yorkshire Terrier Club, an institution belonging to the South of England; in the North, the points vary somewhat, especially in color."

Rather than give the whole Standard that Mr. Randall provides Mr. Compton, we will just give those points that differ from Mr. Coombs. Under *General Appearance*—"the carriage being very upright, and having an important air." Head had now changed measurement from breadth to length, as it says; "nor too long in muzzle" and added to *Head*, "on no account must the tan on the head extend on to the neck." All references to dark, sooty or gray being intermingled with the tan have been collected and phrased as, "nor must there be any sooty or dark hairs intermingled with any of the tan." No mention is made of the hair under the chin.

"*Ears*—small V-shaped and carried semi-erect. *Eyes*—have acquired a "sharp terrier expression," rather than "a sharp intelligent expression."

"*Coat*—The hair on body as long as possible, and perfectly straight (not wavy), glossy like silk, and of a fine silky texture. Colour, a dark steel-blue (not silver-blue) extending from occiput, or back of skull, to the root of the tail, and on no account mingled with fawn, bronze, or dark hairs." Thus, the texture has been described in fuller length. "Flossy" has become "glossy" and "not woolly" has been dropped. The wording has acquired a highbrow tone by adding "occiput."

Legs have added a new measure: "Tan not extending higher on the fore legs than the elbow, nor on the hind legs than the stifle." *Tail* follows Mrs. Mallock's description.

Inserted as a separate clause: "*Tan*—All tan hair should be darker at the roots than in the middle, shading to a still lighter tan at the tips."

"*Weight*—Three classes: 5 lbs. and under; 7 lbs. and under but over 5 lbs.; over 7 lbs." The point value given:

```
Quantity and length of coat . . . . . . . . . . . . . . . . . . . . . . 15
Quality and texture of coat  . . . . . . . . . . . . . . . . . . . . . . 10
Richness of tan on head and legs . . . . . . . . . . . . . . . . . 15
Color of hair on body  . . . . . . . . . . . . . . . . . . . . . . . . . 15
Head . . 10, Eyes . . 5, Ears . . 5, Legs and feet. . . . . . .  5
Tail, carriage of 5, Mouth. . . . . . . . . . . . . . . . . . . . . . .  5
Formation and general appearance  . . . . . . . . . . . . . . . . 10
```

Now the gentleman from the North held with the points as "Symmetry and general appearance, 20; quality and quantity of coat on head, 15; quality and quantity of coat on back, 15; tan, 15; head, 10; eyes, 5; mouth, 5; ears, 5; legs and feet, 5; tail, 5."

The Northerners also stuck with a standard running generally as put forth by Mr. Coombs. The texture has become "which should be glossy like silk (not woolly)." Their dogs, from the birthplace of the Yorkshire Terrier, remain bright steel-blue. Both Mrs. Mallock and Mr. Coombs imported their stock primarily from the North and obviously held with the breed's originators and early fanciers.

Mr. Compton finishes off his article with: "The Yorkshire Terrier fancy is well supplied with specialist clubs, including The Yorkshire Terrier Club, The Halifax and District Y.T Club, The Y.T. Club of

Scotland, The Bolton and District Y.T. Club, and The Manchester and District Y.T. Club. Mr. F. Randall is the Honorary Secretary of the first named, which was formed in 1897, and has done a great deal for the breed, especially in giving a healthier tone to the show ring. It is under the Presidentship of the Countess of Aberdeen, and has passed from the beaten track by recently electing two lady members as judges."

The workers and weavers were about to find their social class carried little weight as the Dames of high degree and fanciers of light and leading took up their pet.

The Manual of Toy Dogs and Their Treatment by Mrs. Leslie Williams, copyrighted 1904, and updated 1910; third edition 1913, has the: "Points of the Yorkshire Terrier as laid down by the Yorkshire Terrier Club, Secretary Mr. F. W. Randall, 'The Clone,' Hampton-on-Thames." It is the same as given by Mr. Compton except that it now states: "Colour, a dark steel-blue (not silver blue)." And then before "the value of points in judging," comes: "*Silver Yorkshires*—points identical with those of the standard Yorkshire, as described above, except colouring, which should be as follows: *Back*—silver. *Head*—pale tan or straw colour. *Muzzle* and *Legs*—light tan. *Ears*—a shade darker tan."

Silver was never a desired color as can be demonstrated by the early write-ups of winning dogs. When bright steel blue was replaced by dark steel blue, one of the breed's original rules established by the originators of the breed was violated. A course was laid that would lead to black Yorkies with tans intermingled with sooty, gray or black hairs. For the use of "dark" was to define the depth of color desired. The point remains that "bright" more lucidly illustrates what was originally desired. Bright gives illumination to steel blue showing that it should reflect light.

It would seem likely that the General Meeting of the Yorkshire Terrier Club in London, January 5, 1911, was a very lively encounter. When the last of the old guard fell before a hail of words from the new recruits to the breed, a new standard was drawn up. The pet dog of the north, became the Toy dog of the south.

The same Standard accepted and approved by the Kennel Club was accepted and approved by the American Kennel Club from 1912 until April 12, 1966. It continues as the Standard approved by the Canadian Kennel Club.

AKC STANDARD FROM 1912 TO 1966

General Appearance—Should be that of a long-coated toy terrier, the coat hanging quite straight and evenly down each side, a parting extending from the nose to the end of the tail. The animal should be very compact and neat, the carriage being very upright, and having an important air. The general outline should convey the existence of a vigorous and well-proportioned body.

Head—Should be rather small and flat, not too prominent or round in the skull, nor too long in the muzzle, with a perfect black nose. The fall on the head to be long, of a rich golden tan, deeper in color at the sides of the head about the ear roots, and on the muzzle where it should be very long. The hair on the chest a rich bright tan. On no account must the tan on the head extend on to the neck, nor must there be any sooty or dark hair intermingled with any of the tan.

Eyes—Medium, dark and sparkling, having a sharp, intelligent expression, and placed so as to look directly forward. They should not be prominent, and the edge of the eyelids should be of a dark color.

Ears—Small, V-shaped, and carried semierect, or erect, and not far apart, covered with short hair, color to be of a very deep rich tan.

Mouth—Perfectly even, with teeth as sound as possible. An animal having lost any teeth through accident not a fault, providing the jaws are even.

Body—Very compact, and a good loin. Level on the top of the back.

Coat—The hair on body moderately long and perfectly straight (not wavy), glossy like silk, and of a fine silky texture. Color, a dark steel blue (not silver blue) extending from the occiput (or back of skull) to the root of tail, and on no account mingled with fawn, bronze or dark hairs.

Legs—Quite straight, well covered with hair of a rich golden tan a few shades lighter at the ends than at the roots, not extending higher on the forelegs than the elbow, nor on the hind legs than the stifle.

Feet—As round as possible, and the toenails black.

Tail—Cut to medium length; with plenty of hair, darker blue in color than the rest of the body, especially at the end of the tail, and carried a little higher than the level of the back.

Tan—All tan hair should be darker at the roots than in the middle, shading to a still lighter tan at the tips.

	Points
Formation and terrier appearance	15
Color of hair on body	15
Richness of tan on head and legs	15
Quality and texture of coat	10
Quantity and length of coat	10
Head	10
Mouth	5
Legs and feet	5
Ears	5
Eyes	5
Tail (carriage of)	5
Total	100

With exception that a specification of "Weight up to 7 lbs." has been added, and the point specifications at the end of the standard have been dropped, these remain the requirements called for in the English Standard today.

In 1966, the Yorkshire Terrier Club of America drew up a new Standard, approved by the Board of Directors of the American Kennel Club, and this Standard—reproduced on the pages that follow—is the one that applies in this country today. It was the hope of dedicated fanciers of the breed that the updating and rearranging of some of the wording of the old Standard and the adding of specifications on the color of puppies would benefit the breed. With hindsight, however, we now see that these hopes have not materialized. It remains, alas, that to fully comprehend the Standard, one must be aware of the meanings behind its words.

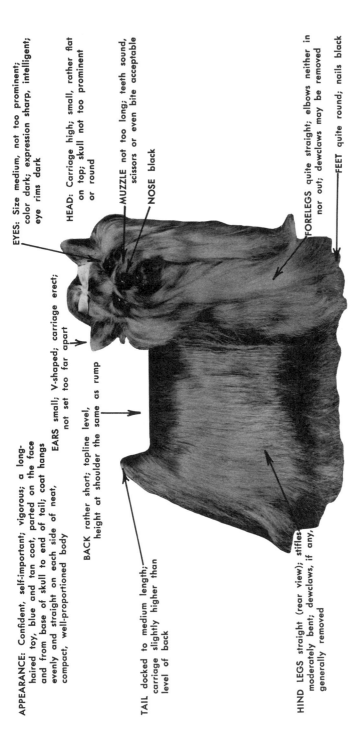

APPEARANCE: Confident, self-important; vigorous; a long-haired toy, blue and tan coat, parted on the face and from base of skull to end of tail; coat hangs evenly and straight on each side of neat, compact, well-proportioned body

BACK rather short; topline level, height at shoulder the same as rump

TAIL docked to medium length; carriage slightly higher than level of back

HIND LEGS straight (rear view); stifles moderately bent; dewclaws, if any, generally removed

COLORS: Puppies are born black/tan. Adult blue is steel blue (not silver nor mingled with fawn, bronze or black hairs). Tan hair is darker at roots, shading lighter to tips (no sooty or black hair with tan). Blue extends over body from back of neck to tail root. Hair on tail darker blue, especially at end. Headfall rich, golden tan, deeper at sides, ear roots and on muzzle. Ears a deep, rich, tan (tan should not extend down back of neck). Chest, legs, a bright, rich tan, not extending above elbows or above stifles

EYES: Size medium, not too prominent; color dark; expression sharp, intelligent; eye rims dark

HEAD: Carriage high; small, rather flat on top; skull not too prominent or round

EARS small; V-shaped; carriage erect; not set too far apart

MUZZLE not too long; teeth sound, scissors or even bite acceptable

NOSE black

COAT quality, texture and quantity of prime importance: Texture glossy, fine glossy, silky; body coat long, straight (not wavy); may be trimmed to floor length; the headfall can be tied with one or two bows; muzzle hair long; hair on ear tips trimmed; hair on feet may be trimmed

FORELEGS quite straight; elbows neither in nor out; dewclaws may be removed

FEET quite round; nails black

WEIGHT: Must not exceed 7 pounds

Visualization of the Yorkshire Terrier standard.—Courtesy, *Dog Standards Illustrated*, Howell Book House Inc.

104

6

Official AKC Standard for the Yorkshire Terrier

General Appearance—That of a long-haired toy terrier whose blue and tan coat is parted on the face and from the base of the skull to the end of the tail and hangs evenly and quite straight down each side of body. The body is neat, compact and well-proportioned. The dog's high head carriage and confident manner should give the appearance of vigor and self-importance.

Head—Small and rather flat on top, the skull not too prominent or round, the muzzle not too long, with the bite neither undershot nor overshot and teeth sound. Either scissors bite or level bite is acceptable. The nose is black. Eyes are medium in size and not too prominent; dark in color and sparkling with a sharp intelligent expression. Eye rims are dark. Ears are small, V-shaped carried erect and set not too far apart.

Body—Well proportioned and very compact. The back is rather short, the back line level, with height at shoulder the same as at the rump.

Legs and Feet—Forelegs should be straight, elbows neither in nor out. Hind legs straight when viewed from behind, but stifles are moderately bent when viewed from the sides. Feet are round with black toenails. Dewclaws, if any, are generally removed from the hind legs. Dewclaws on the forelegs may be removed.

Tail—Docked to a medium length and carried slightly higher than the level of the back.

Coat—Quality, texture and quantity of coat are of prime importance. Hair is glossy, fine and silky in texture. Coat on the body moderately long and perfectly straight (not wavy). It may be trimmed to floor length to give ease of movement and a neater appearance, if desired. The fall on the head is long, tied with one bow in center of head or parted in the middle and tied with two bows. Hair on muzzle is very long. Hair should be trimmed short on tips of ears and may be trimmed on feet to give them a neat appearance.

Colors—Puppies are born black and tan and are normally darker in body color, showing intermingling of black hair in the tan until they are matured. Color of hair on body and richness of tan on head and legs are of prime importance in *adult dogs*, to which the following color requirements apply:
BLUE: Is a dark steel-blue, not a silver-blue and not mingled with fawn, bronze or black hairs.
TAN: All tan hair is darker at the roots than in the middle, shading to still lighter tan at the tips. There should be no sooty or black hair intermingled with any of the tan.
Color on Body—The blue extends over the body from back of neck to root of tail. Hair on tail is a darker blue, especially at end of tail.
Headfall—A rich golden tan, deeper in color at sides of head, at ear roots and on the muzzle, with ears a deep rich tan. Tan color should not extend down on back of neck.
Chest and Legs—A bright, rich tan, not extending above the elbow on the forelegs nor above the stifle on the hind legs.

Weight—Must not exceed seven pounds.

Approved April 12, 1966.

7

In-Depth Study
of the Standard

THE YORKSHIRE TERRIER'S type is embodied in the points of the Standard that distinguish it from other purebred dogs. The English Standard is slightly different in wording from the American Standard—differences we shall note further on in this chapter—but both desire the same type of Yorkshire Terrier.

In the United States, it is the present American Kennel Club approved Standard that we—whether breeder, exhibitor or judge—must accept as guide. The question of whether it is a good set of rules, clearly worded, setting forth the ideal model, will remain. A new Standard, or revision of the present, might steady the breed's flow, but past experience doesn't present an airtight case for such thinking. Our better course would seem to lie in looking into the reasons and thoughts behind the wording of the Standard.

The points in *General Appearance* are more clearly defined in the rest of the Standard. It is well, however, to place them mentally before us before going further into the master plan of the Yorkie's framework.

General Appearance—That of a long-haired Toy Terrier whose blue and tan coat is parted on the face and from the base of the skull to the end of the tail, and hangs evenly and quite straight down each side of body. The body is neat, compact and well-proportioned. The dog's high head carriage and confident manner should give the appearance of vigor and self-importance.

A true Yorkshire must meet these requirements—if it fails, it is pointless to study it into the finer points of the Standard. They contain in themselves the general description of the breed's characteristics—though words have been shuffled—that have served since the first specifications were set down to differentiate purebred dogs from run-of-the-mill canines.

To begin with, it is a Toy Terrier. The word "Toy" does not mean it is a plaything, even though all Yorkies enjoy playing. Toy here explains that it is to be small—diminutive—but still a Terrier.

Its body is sketched in—neat (trim, tidy, orderly), compact and well-proportioned.

Its color, with no ifs or ands, is blue and tan. Its hair is long and quite straight down each side of the body. Only a silk-satin textured coat will fill this rule.

Finally, there is its temperament. It carries its head high, showing pride. Its confident manner gives it an appearance of self-importance and pride.

Head

If we look back to Mr. Dalziel's description of 1878, and *Standard and Points of Judging the Yorkshire* of 1891, we find excellent examples of how rules laid down in the early stages still form part of the present Standard.

Dalziel: "Head is rather small, rather flat on the crown."

Coombs: "Head should be rather small and flat, not too prominent or round in skull, rather broad at the muzzle."

The topline of the Yorkshire Terrier's small head—as viewed from the side—descends from the highest point of the occiput over the skull to the muzzle ending at the nostrils in a rather flat line. The Yorkshire Terrier does not have a pronounced stop—it does have a slight one.

The Standard specifies "the skull not too prominent or round"—meaning that it is not to be a bumpy skull, nor is it to be apple-headed.

At one time in its patterning, the problem facing Yorkshire Terrier breeders was the length of the head. The long and short of it has now

Beautiful head.

Large ears, poorly set.

Faulty—bat (rounded) ears.

been resolved with muzzle "not too long." Luckily, although the words have gone through shifting positions, the Yorkie's head description has held pretty close to the original rules laid down by its originators. It is rare to see an apple-headed Yorkie with its accompanying very short muzzle—the so-called "doll-faced" Yorkie. Nor are there very many with the long muzzle, which are generally down-faced. The men who established the points of the breed were aware that early ancestors of the Yorkies carried these unwanted points, and with maintenance of their rules the genes for these faults have been nearly retired from its makeup.

The Yorkshire's muzzle is not snipey, it is definitely wider than narrow. A snipey muzzle is pointed and weak. On this point, you can tuck away information that has been dropped out, breadth does play a part in the shape of your Yorkie's foremost extension.

The Yorkshire Terrier's earlier definitions called for a level bite, but as the realization came that the type of bite can be inherited, breeders felt that this was teetering on the rim a little too close. To control (as much as possible) the inheritance of bites being neither overshot nor undershot, scissors bite *or* level was allowed.

The best test for your Yorkshire Terrier's bite is the line and meeting of the animal's upper and lower jawbones. The jawbones, when the mouth is closed, should fit together in a straight line forward. The upper jawbone should fit closely over the lower jawbone. If the jawbones do not fit together, or the upper jawbone does not overlap the lower jawbone as it extends forward, you will obtain a wry mouth, lower jaw tilted from one side to another.

If the front teeth of the lower jaw are overlapping or projecting beyond the front teeth of the upper jaw when the mouth is closed, you will have an undershot bite in the manner of a Bulldog. If the front teeth of the upper jaw are overlapping the front teeth of the under jaw when the mouth is closed, you have acquired an overshot bite à la "Andy Gump."

Subtracted from the Standard in 1966 was a section most breeders would like to see restored: "An animal having lost any teeth through accident not a fault, providing the jaws are even." (This is still in the English Standard.) In fact, most knowledgeable breeders would be happy to carry this one step farther and have it say: "Teeth lost through age or accident not a fault, provided the jaws are even."

Before one hastily cries that either instance is a result of negligence, one should know the facts. Nobody ever told the Yorkie that it wasn't a sure-footed mountain goat. A number of Yorkies have found themselves on the floor with happily no more damage than a hole in their dentition. And have you ever tried to break up a Yorkie battle? The little silky-coated demons can hang on until one loosens a tooth. This doesn't stop their fight, but it leaves one party with a missing tooth.

Good care of a Yorkshire includes keeping its teeth free of tartar. But sooner or later, as they age, they'll need to have their teeth cleaned by a veterinarian. With their small jaws, this usually means an anesthetic to protect the Yorkie from ending up with a dislocated jaw. All Yorkshire Terrier owners approach the thought of an anesthetic with trepidation. Ninety-nine and nine tenths of the time all is well. But the one tenth, the time that you're told *your* dog didn't come out of the anesthetic, just doesn't make you remember all that have. Therefore, the risk of having an older dog's teeth cleaned or allowing them to fall out, should be strictly the exhibitor's choice. Some fine dogs—dogs that in appearance were models of what the breed should be, or who represented excellent potential as breeding stock—have been lost to future generations through the Yorkie's delicate response to anesthesia.

At the same time, it must be recognized that a rotting tooth can be risky to the animal's health. An obvious case of poor care should be considered a more serious fault than a tooth lost through accident.

Nose

"The nose is black." The only change from the old Standard in this is the dropping of the word "perfect" from in front of black. A dog whose nose is not black shows the breakdown of pigmentation and should be strongly faulted. Because of the strong emergence in recent years of this heretofore unreported problem, breeders, judges and buyers should be especially watchful against these animals.

Eyes

"Eyes are medium in size and not too prominent; dark in color and sparkling with a sharp intelligent expression. Eye rims are dark."

In one earlier standard, a specification called for the eyes to have a "sharp terrier expression"—a requirement of rather questionable utility. For example, the Bull Terrier Standard wants an eye with "a piercing glint'' and ''well sunken,'' while the Dandie Dinmont Standard calls for an eye that is ''large, full, round.''

A round eye gives a Yorkie a quite woebegone expression, far from what is wanted. And a well-sunken eye will not show a Yorkie's mischief, deviltry and keenness. The Yorkie's eyes minus their sparkling sharp intelligent expression take away a large piece of the breed's identity.

In Yorkshires with an extremely red-haired head one is likely to find the lighter eye rim and, almost always, light eyes. Dark eyes, medium in size, help to give him his keen, bright expression and all should steer clear of light eyes or light eye-rimmed dogs.

Eye placement was dropped from the new Standard. The previous Standard contained wording, still in the British Standard, that specified: ''And placed so as to look directly forward.'' It would be good to reinsert this, for it is one of the terrier characteristics of the Yorkshire Terrier.

Ears

The Standard concludes Head specifications with: *''Ears are small, V-shaped and set not too far apart.''* Such a short sentence, but what a load underlies it. The genius that added the beastly word ''too'' should be made to realize that too many toos have too often led to too much woe. Before the present Standard, the specification had simply been ''not far apart.'' The British Standard still has it that way. The addition of the word ''too'' changes the whole picture by allowing for any kind of interpretation.

The Yorkshire Terrier should have small V-shaped ears. They should not be round at their tips, nor bat-shaped like a French Bulldog's. They are carried erect, and when excited or at attention, carried higher. Many Yorkies, when gaiting, will flick one ear rearward, keeping a mental check on what foe might be advancing on them.

Although this is not covered in the Yorkie Standard, the ears should have quite thin leather (outer cartilage of the ear), though with enough strength to keep them erect. Thick leather leads to semierect or drop ears.

Low-set ears take away from a Yorkshire Terrier's alert expression, one of the breed's identifying points. Tying long hair from them into the topknot to make them appear higher set, or not too far apart, should not fool anyone. The animal's ears remain stationary and useless.

The size of the ear should receive a good deal of appreciative regard. Yorkies' ears were cropped until cropping was outlawed in Great Britain in 1895. The ancestors that went into the production of the Yorkshire Terrier all had large ears and they are dominant genetically to small ears. While in a well-cultivated adult Yorkshire, with ears properly trimmed and dressed with golden feathers, the shape of the ear is barely visible, no breeder should ever forget that the ears do add up in the total of a prosperous look to the head.

Body

The Standard calls for *"Body—Well proportioned and very compact. The back is rather short, the back line level, with height at shoulder the same as at the rump."* (To this add the description of "neat" from General Appearance.)

The use of the word "rather" before "short" is quite senseless. How can it be "very compact" if it is *rather* (defined as "in some degree") short backed? The Yorkie's body is well-proportioned; the word picture projected should be one that portrays the terminology of the body's description, namely that the topline is to be perfectly level. The length of the back is to be in relation to the height at the shoulders and the rump so that the animal appears basically square.

A common mistake that is made is illustrated by this quote from a magazine: ''A Yorkie should look square, which means that the legs should be the same length as the back, giving room for length of coat.'' Such a dog has either no body between its back or legs, or it has a long back to equal its leg length and overlooked body. It is the Yorkshire's body AND leg length that square it against its short back.

The Yorkshire's back is a straight, level line from its shoulders to the set-on of the tail; i.e., the rump. The less loin between the back rib and the hip bones, the better. With a short loin, it is more likely to achieve the desired level topline.

The short loin should have breadth and well-developed muscles. The loin is the dog's pivotal point, and strength aids in the ability to make rapid changes in direction—whether forward, reverse, up or down. An underdeveloped, long, narrow loin shows up as a weak point in a topline.

Well-proportioned body and good balance. Proper head and expression with small ears. Unmistak-ably feminine stamp. *William Brown*

The lay of the shoulders is not mentioned in the standard but, as they underlie its back, they need to be considered. Good shoulders, well placed, are very necessary to obtain freedom of movement, which will show in the straightness of a Yorkie's backline when it is gaiting or posing. Good shoulders form the correct foundation for a sound forefront. They help to shorten the back and form the correct base for the neck to flow smoothly into the backline.

Looking down onto a Yorkie's back, the topline seen from side to side is reasonably broad. Its chest should have a good spring of ribs. This curvature of ribs, along with a comparatively wide front and depth between its forelegs, allows for good heart and lung capacity. This latter point was very important when it was used as a ratter or varmint hunter and often went underground or swam through water. Though few Yorkies engage in such activity now, they are a very vigorous and robust breed and still need the heart and lung room.

Legs and Feet

An unsoundness of legs, fore or hind, will detract from the Yorkshire's general carriage and topline, in motion or when it is standing at attention, most likely wondering whether the onlooker knows as much about it as it is sure it knows about itself.

The Yorkshire Terrier belongs to the digging terrier family. Its forelegs are straight, with the elbows close to the chest, neither in nor out. The lower forelegs do toe out slightly, like a Cairn Terrier, so that when digging the dirt will fly out to the sides and not pile under it. The forelegs should be medium in length and strongly muscled.

The Yorkshire's hindlegs, whether in motion or standing still, are straight, with the hocks parallel, not close together or cow-hocked.

Its hindlegs are broad across the pelvic area. If the pelvis is narrow, the Yorkie's rear gait will make it look as if both hindlegs were attached in one place. The upper thighs should carry a firm muscular pack.

The Yorkie is to have a moderate bend at the stifles, viewed from the side. Lack of angulation at the stifle causes lack of drive and short strides increase wear and tear on the ''kneecaps.'' Medium strides that bear the rear end at an equal level with the fore-end are your desire.

The hocks on the Yorkshire Terrier should be well angulated to give it power and good movement. They, along with the back pastern, should be short. Ideally, the hocks should come to just about a line drawn down from the rearmost point of the animal's body. Hocks too far to the rear give a loss of control in the rear-end action.

Good movement and soundness are primarily dependent upon having bones of the right size, and in the right place. The bones in its legs should be medium in girth, taking into measure that what fits a two-pound Yorkie is not suited to a seven-pound Yorkie.

With proper hindlegs, a Yorkie will move with verve, and pose without upsetting the level line of its back. Its height at the rump will be the same as at the shoulders and it will retain its neat, compact and well-proportioned aspect.

The majority of Yorkshires have front feet larger than their rear feet, as do several of their Scotch cousins. The feet are round and should be tight, with the toes not spread apart. The pads should be well-formed and firm.

The toenails are often overlooked, but should be checked to see that they are black. In the hazy past of the Yorkie's ancestry, some animal contributed white toenails to its get. The men who drew up the rules for the breed knew it, and made a point to include specification of black toenails in its pattern. It's a minor point, but should be of concern to breeders, awakening them to the fact that it has this gene in its storehouse. (Quite a few Yorkies are born with one or more white toenails, but by maturity they will have turned black. If not, you have a clue that you have an animal with the ability to pass on white markings.)

This section of the Standard states that dewclaws are generally removed from the hindlegs, and may be removed from the forelegs. Remove them on all legs, or you are likely to catch a comb on one and have a sore-legged Yorkshire Terrier while the damage heals.

Neck

Before continuing our journey through the approved Standard, we note that there is one part of the Yorkshire Terrier's body that is not referred to, and that is its neck. Like all quadrupeds, it *does* have a connection between its head and shoulders.

When it was first being established as a separate part of the canine sphere, it was its ratting ability that was extolled. The little Yorkshire

Terrier of the working man grabbed the rat and, with a quick snap of its head, dispatched the rodent. It takes a neck to move the head in this snatching action.

The Yorkshire of today still carries this ability, though its chances of being entered in a ratting contest are almost nil. Still, it does shake its toys in the same manner, and a specimen with a thin, long neck is likely to find itself indisposed with displaced verterbrae—a sort of doggy whiplash.

Under these circumstances, the best type of neck for a Yorkshire should be a muscular one, without coarseness. Moderately short, but not so short as to appear clumsy. It should have sufficient neck length to carry its head proudly, adding to its elegant appearance and contributing to a well-proportioned square body. The neck should flow smoothly into the neckline.

Do not be deceived into believing that the Yorkshire Standard calls for "a long, elegant reach of neck." The change in the Standard from "the carriage being very upright and having an important air" to "The dog's high head carriage and confident manner should give the appearance of vigor and self-importance" has led some people astray. This change only signifies that it is proud, bold and forward in its carriage.

Tail

To resume with what *is* in the approved Standard, we come to: *"Tail—Docked to a medium length and carried slightly higher than the level of the back."*

Many a Yorkshire worthy of sympathy has found itself looked at with disfavor for having too short a tail when, in reality, it is not its fault at all. Whoever docked it either made it too short or—having no guide to go by—docked it to what was medium of the length of the tail with which the puppy arrived into this world.

Obviously, medium meaning middle, one wants a tail that is neither too short or too long. Most long-time breeders have their veterinarians dock tails to one eighth to one quarter inch past the tan on the underside, giving a tail length that at the animal's mature size will vary from one and a half to two and a half inches (from the set-on of the tail to its tip).

The set-on of the tail is actually a greater concern, for this it is born with. A Yorkshire Terrier's tail-set should be high on the croup (the back part of the back, above the hindlegs). The tail is the extension of the vertebrae that make up its spine. In an animal where it is desired to have a level back, the croup is nearly parallel to the horizon. A rounding-off of the rump, with a low tail-set, makes for a roach-back appearance.

The Standard prescribes that the tail be carried "slightly higher than the level of the back." A Yorkshire with its tail tucked between its legs looks like it is cringing and fearful of the world, or belongs at home in a sickbed. Your Yorkshire is a stiff gentleman. When encountering a newcomer, it brings its tail upright while the question of territorial rights and friendly relations are established—an accord reached or the battleline drawn!

Avoid breeding together dogs with low tail-sets; you want a Yorkshire that can carry its tail above the topline while gaiting, or drop it straight down in repose. You will, of course, be chancing a too-gay tail. But better an animal with gay tail whose general appearance suggests the Standard's prescription of "confidence, vigor and self-importance" than one whose unseen tail makes it appear shy, weak, and of no consequence.

Coat

The Yorkshire Terrier becomes a unique breed of dog by virtue of its outer covering—its cloak of shining blue and bright gold silk, whose general outline conveys the existence of a vigorous and well-proportioned body carried with self-importance. The dressing of the head's long, bright gold hairs allows the Yorkie to parade its sharp, intelligent terrier spirit.

The Yorkie is alone among purebred dogs in its demand for metallic colors of gleaming radiance displayed through hairs of lustrous spun silk. A Yorkie with impure, weak colors—hair incapable of naturally reflecting light rays, or hair of thicker grade—can never achieve the unique, glowing coloring that truly typifies a model of the breed.

The prime points of a Yorkie's coat are its texture and its colors. The two are equally important, for without one or the other, the Yorkie has lost type. The texture and colors cooperate to produce the animal desired in the Standard.

Fully mature individual showing full face furnishings. Compare this strongly masculine specimen with the bitch on page 114.   *E. Shafer*

We will here explore these points in four sections: texture, colors, transition from newly born to adult, and how the color is acquired.

1. *Coat Texture*

The Standard states *"Quality, texture and quantity of coat are of prime importance."* The Yorkshire's "quantity" of hair is long—and of a density that hangs flat, evenly against the body. The long hair should never be so thick as to completely hide the outline of the underlying body. Its length should not impede the dog's ability to show off its carriage. To this purpose, the body coat—if desired—may be trimmed. If the owner does not trim, he assumes the risk that the impediment may deter chances of higher placement in showing his dogs.

The long hair falls from all parts of the head and is longest on the muzzle. The hair on the skull is tied up so as to better show the sharp intelligent eyes and the ear carriage that help express the Yorkie's character.

The hair hangs straight and totally free of wave. In the specification under General Appearance that the coat hangs "quite straight," the word *quite* is used in the sense of *completely*. In middle English, quite meant "free, rid of" and in Latin "freed."

The factor necessary for straight hair is inheritable. When seen through a microscope, cross sections of individual hair strands look round, oval or flat. A round-shaped hair is straight. Scientists have found that curly hair is usually a dominant trait; straight is usually recessive because it is masked by a more dominant characteristic.

The undesired waviness is usually found in the light silver Yorkies, but has begun to be seen in black woollies and gray cottony-coated Yorkshires, too. In this reference to waviness we are not talking of the little left over from poor grooming when the "crackers" (i.e. wraps) are removed, but one that runs through the coat in long, horizontal, wavy lines.

The feet and ears grow an equal quantity of hair, but are trimmed. The standard states that feet *may* be trimmed for neatness. The movement of a Yorkie's legs is often only visible in the placement of the feet, and long hair on them can cause false illusions. Also, untrimmed feet can often harbor foreign objects that can cause injury or infection.

The thick, heavy coat on this 3½ month-old puppy indicates that it will not show correct visual color at adulthood.

These silky-coated puppies are four and three months old respectively. Their coats appear thinner than that of the puppy in the photo at left. However, as adults they will carry thick, long coats of the correct fine, silky, glossy texture.

A wavy coat will become visible at an early age and generally portends a light silver color in the adult. This dog's wavy coat is still silky as indicated by the reflected light.

A straight, fine, silky coat.   *Glenview Studio*

The ears should be trimmed on the tips. The Standard does not leave this point open to personal choice. The trimmed ear shows the shape, size and ear placement. An untrimmed ear subtracts from the head's total appearance, and from a structural point of view—long, heavy hair growth on the eartip is likely to bring it down to a drop or semierect ear.

The long "quantity" of hair is recessive to short hair. A Yorkie with hair that is short due to neglect or illness is one matter, but a Yorkie with a short silky coat should be considered as uncharacteristic.

The length of the hair depends (aside from care) on its quality. The correct individual hair strands of a Yorkie are of a *fine* grade.

Hairs are produced by glands situated in the inner layers of the skin. These glands secrete the protein called *keratin* that forms the hair. The hair has an inner and outer core. The quality of the hair (fine, medium or thick) is determined by the hair-producing glands and the manner in which the hair passes through the hair follicle cells. Hairs with thick outer cores are heavy and dull, for the extent to which they can refract light is diminished by the thickness and roughness of the outer layer.

The Yorkie's coat is made up of fine, silken hairs. In this era of manmade fibers, few know the true feel of silk as spun by the silkworm munching its way through mulberry leaves. Silk is cool and strong. This coolness can still be felt in the desired silken-haired coat; when the hair is laid over your hand, it will feel cool, and not warm your hand as will the wrong-textured coat. It was because of this cooling quality that clothes for tropical countries were made of silk rather than wool. As for its strength, this can be tested by taking a thread of silk, a strand of wool, and a thread of 100 percent cotton, and trying to break each in half. The wool will part first, and then the cotton, but you may cut your hand before you part the silk thread. The strength of the fine, silky hair (as opposed to the woolly or cottony coat) allows it to grow to proper length with the quality that maintains it without snarling, matting or splitting.

The Yorkie's fine silky coat is *glossy* in texture. Around 1876, Dr. Gordon Staples wrote:

> There are one or two things remarkable about the coat and feathers of a well-bred Yorkshire. First, its extreme length. Secondly, its great straightness. The least approach to a curl of a Yorkshire would prove fatal to its success in the show ring. Thirdly, the quality of the feather.

Ch. Wildweir Tabaaho, bred and owned by Nancy Donovan, showing the typical, immature face furnishings on a year-old dog.   *Martin Booth*

Ch. Wildweir's Wicked Countess at five months.

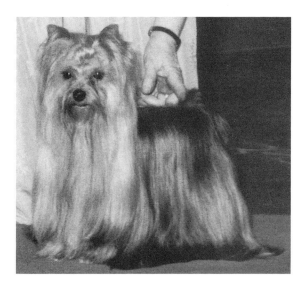

Ch. Wildweir's Wicked Countess at maturity showing the full show coat so highly prized in the breed.

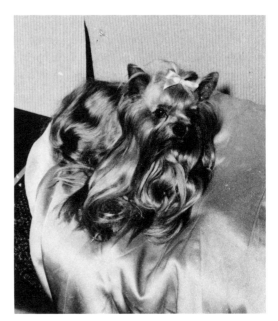

In an interesting, graphic comparison a fine, silky coat is displayed on satin.

The look of a full show coat on a dog in full stride.

Ch. Galfred's Joker's Wild, owned by Gail Rasmussen, showing the normal coat growth of an adolescent (16 months). *DiGiacomo*

It is soft and silky—it is flat down to the sides. And, as the little things sport and frolic about the carpet and engage in mimic warfare, the feathers ripple upon them and this combined with its sheen and color gives these Toys the appearance of being clothed in little jackets of flowing water.

Originally, the word used in the Yorkie Standard to describe the surface of its coat was "*flossy,*" which comes from floss silk. This silk is described as "soft, downy and made of the untwisted thread from unreelable silk fibers."

The word in the Standard has been changed to "*glossy,*" defined as "having luster or shine, polished." Luster in turn is "to shine or have sheen with brilliancy, especially from reflected light."

The Yorkie coat should look like satin, a smooth silk woven with a glossy face. A coat that does not have a polished, shining surface is not a glossy-textured coat. It cannot reflect and refract light, essential requirements for providing the visible metallic gleaming colors of a Yorkie.

The hair's length, fineness, silkiness and glossy qualities are all factors in the transmission of its colors to the human eye.

2. *Colors*

ADULT COAT COLOR

The coat color for the adult Yorkie is set down in the Standard as:

Color of hair on body and richness of tan on head and legs are of prime importance in Adult dogs, to which the following color requirements apply:

BLUE: Is a dark steel-blue, not a silver-blue and not mingled with fawn, bronzy or black hairs.
TAN: All tan hair is darker at the roots than in the middle, shading to still lighter tan at the tips. There should be no sooty or black hair intermingled with any of the tan.

The difficulty in determining what the colors specified in the Standard look like, and how they are produced, has been a major stumbling block in the understanding of the Yorkie's adult coloring.

Defining color is based on the eyes of the beholder. It is determined by the individual's perception of light rays reflected to his eyes.

All interpretations by an individual are the net result of his environmental learning and binocular efficiency. In childhood, you learn that leaves are green, the sky is blue, newly fallen snow is white and moonless nights are black. Color names follow the current fads: last year's "dusty rose" becomes this year's "gray-pink." Your occupation, hobbies and place of habitation all influence your name for each color hue.

The individual's discernment of color involves *hue, brilliance and saturation,* and depends on the light source. In speaking of color, various terms such as *dark, medium* or *light* designate differing degrees of vividness of hue. This vividness is also determined by the light's radiancy.

The Standard specifies that the adult (over twelve months, i.e. one year) Yorkshire Terrier's body coat is a dark steel-blue, darker on the tail, especially on the tip. The *hue* required is the primary color blue. The saturation point of the blue is *dark*—that is differing in degree by being higher or lower than medium blue, but minus any approach to blackness.

The word "steel" is used to show *brilliance.* The dark blue is to reflect light rays. Black, for example, is destitute of light, or incapable of naturally reflecting it. The blue color is to shine, to have luster, gloss, a metallic sheen—as of a piece of polished steel.

As a slight diversion here, it is interesting to note some of the images that "dark steel-blue" has brought to mind. Here's one:

"The old timers said it was the color you saw when you looked down a clean gun barrel. That's all right for Sheffield, where they make gun barrels, but we don't have the same opportunity down South (England), and as far as I'm concerned, the last thing I'd do would be to look down a gun barrel."

Our sentiment exactly! Anyway, modern gun barrels are made out of alloyed steel. Here's another comparison, less lethal:

"A deep shade of metal like the blade of a knife, not stainless steel but the old-fashioned knife we used to have—the blade of which when polished gave a blue shade."

Can you imagine a group of Yorkie fanciers encircling a judge, making their point with a flourish, that their specimen most closely resembles the knives they are wielding?

The Standard prescribes that the adult Yorkshire Terrier is to have a headfall that is *"a rich golden tan, deeper in color at sides of head at ear roots and on the muzzle, with ears a deep rich tan!''* Chest and legs are ''a bright, rich tan.''

Thus the *hue* required is the color termed tan (red-yellow in hue, of high saturation). The degree of vividness varies from deep to bright. The saturation point of the tan is *rich*, that is abundant in color as opposed to pale in color.

The word ''golden'' is used to show that the tan is to show *brilliance*, with a high degree of ability to reflect light source rays. Refined and polished gold has a metallic gleaming brightness.

The Yorkshire's adult colors are given placement. *''The blue extends over the body from back of neck to root of tail. Hair on the tail is a darker blue, especially at end of tail.''* The requirement for this darker blue on the tail and tip is a safeguard to keep the tan on the underside (not top or sides) of the tail. It also maintains a visible sign that the pigment supply for the blue is kept strong and not weakened, thus allowing the tan to run up into the blue body from the breeches.

The deeper color of the golden tan on the muzzle, sides of head (also above the eyes), base of ears, is at the areas that were tan marks at birth. Their deep richness in tan pigment is necessary to maintain a golden tan throughout the Yorkie's lifespan, and to pass on the genetic ability to supply this need in succeeding generations. Even the palest golden tan should always show this shading of darker gold deposits at these placement points.

The ears are the deepest golden tan. The insides of the ear should always be a rich golden tan. The hairs on the outside of the ear leather are very dark rich golden tan. Close observation on many Yorkies will show an intermingling of blackish, red-brown (sooty) hairs. If these hairs predominate, or if they are black-hued hairs, the transition from black to gold will never develop completely. The dog will invariably fail to assume any visible-to-the-eye blue hue. The best it will do is a grayish-black body color. In some it will extend on to the skull, and even reach down around the eyes, forming a black mask.

The tan *''should not extend down on back of neck.''* The tan on the chest does not extend into the blue body. On the legs it is not to extend *''above the elbow on the forelegs nor above the stifle on the hind legs.''*

These placements make what is termed a saddle pattern. In the case of the Yorkie, this description is of a complete body saddle.

Coloring of the adult Yorkshire Terrier as prescribed by the Standard. Arrow indicates darker color at the tail.

Coloring of the adult Yorkshire Terrier as it actually is. Arrow indicates darker color at the tail.

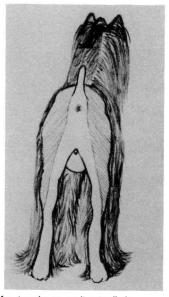
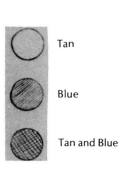

Tan

Blue

Tan and Blue

Coloring of the adult Yorkshire Terrier, front and rear, as it actually is.

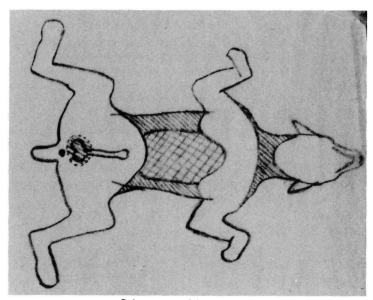

Color pattern of the underside.

The Yorkshire Terrier Standard is deficient in its failure to mention that the average Yorkie's blue color extends from the body around the lower throat and the upper top of the forechest, while the tan covers the underside of the tail, around the vent and the breeching.

On the underside of a Yorkie, on the brisket and midway along the pelvic arc there are blue sections. The rest of the underside is usually tan, lightest at the armpits and belly.

An adult Yorkie may not be a silver-blue, silver being defined as a neutral (minus any approach to whiteness) gray—that is, midway between black and white. The blue body coat may not be intermingled with hairs that are fawn (red-yellow in hue), bronzy (brown, yellowish, red-yellow in hue) or black (devoid of light-reflecting ability, or so dark as to have no distinguishable color). Overlapping of blue-black and reddish tan hairs in the blue coat produce the bronzy coat appearance.

The adult Yorkie's tan may not be intermingled with sooty (brownish-black) or black-hued hairs. Hairs that are grayish-black (lighter pigmented black) are not golden tan and fall under the edict of no black hairs intermingled. Any amount of mingled hairs, other than golden tan hues, takes away from the brilliance of the golden color. Mingled black hairs that form any visible group are obviously signs of impurity of the golden color and should be considered a very bad fault in breeding, or showing.

The adult Yorkie's blue should be a uniform shade of blue. It should not appear patched, striped or half light and half dark. A scratched or injured area will appear darker in its new outgrowth, but is perceivable by its shortened length. For the desired correctly colored Yorkie, the base of the hair shaft is a darker shade of the coat's blue color and this darker shade will show at any parting down to the skin.

The adult Yorkie's tan hair should be darker at the roots than in the middle, shading to a still lighter tan at the tips. This requirement can only be met when the hair is of the required fine quality.

ADULT SKIN COLOR:

The underlying skin has pigmentation of the same color hue as the hair. The head, chest and legs have skin pigment that is light yellowish pink to moderate reddish orange-yellow. The inside of the ear is the same, but the outside pigmentation of the ear leather is a reddish-brown. The body's skin has a pigment that is a light grayish-blue to medium grayish-blue. The pigmentation on top and sides of the tail is medium gray-blue to dark gray-blue.

There is a nearly clear-cut line between the pigmentation on the head at the back of the skull, on the forelegs at the elbow and on the hindlegs at the stifle. On the tail, the line divides the blue, leaving the tan on the underside of the tail.

There may be a band of light, grayish-blue pigment on the lower forechest above the shoulder points and across the underside of the rib cage. This pigmentation will not be a clearly defined area, and may be interspersed with reddish-yellow colored skin.

On the rear end, the Yorkie has reddish-yellow skin pigment on the tail's underside, around the vent, rear of the upper thighs, the breeches and down the outer edge of the inside of the rear legs. The hocks and all other underside areas not already mentioned are light reddish golden-yellow to medium golden red-yellow.

When the golden pigmentation extends beyond or is mixed into the body's pigmentation, the body color will have intermingled fawn hairs.

Darker patches of blue pigmentation will have outgrowing patches of darker blue-hued hairs.

If the skin is injured, the hair scratched or torn out, the healed skin with the early hair growth will be a darker area until it returns to normal.

Very bluish-black or dark grayish-black skin pigment will have hairs that are black or less heavily pigmented grays.

If the body color extends out of its lines into the golden tan areas, the tan will be intermingled with hairs varying from light gray to black.

3. *Transition from Newly Born to Adult*

The Yorkshire Terrier is usually born black with tan points, the tan being on the following places: on the puppy's muzzle; above each eye; base of ear; ear rims; inside of ear; underside of tail (extending midway out from body on uncut tail) around the vent and edge of breechings; on the outside of forelegs, feet and a small way up pastern; on the inside of the forelegs extending from armpit slightly onto the chest wall. There is tan on the outside of rear legs, on paws, and partially up pastern; a fine line extending up to stifle on front; and part of hock on rear side. The inside of the hindleg is tan except for a small blackish V-shaped patch on each upper inside thigh joined by a black bridge across the pelvic arch.

The rest of the underside, except for a black girth around the rear chest and brisket, is tan. The underside of the jaw (though there may be a black patch in the middle of the underside of the lower jaw) and the underside of the throat is tan. The forechest has a rosette at each shoulder point, or a horizontal stripe between them in the black.

The tan on a young Yorkie puppy is a light pale golden tan to a dark rich golden tan. All tan marks may be more or less in extension. They may be perfectly delineated from the black, or be slightly intermingled with blackish hair.

There may be a white star or a small blaze located on the forechest in the tan, or across the black and tan. This is a much looked-for point, as it is an indication that the puppy will probably be a good coat grower in quantity, though not necessarily in quality. It is also an indication that there will be no melanism, or oversupply of pigment.

It is not unusual to find small white marks on one or more toes, or a fine white line on lower forejaw. These will not be visible as an adult. Any such marks should therefore be noted wherever you keep such records, as one is apt to forget which puppy had them after they grow up.

A large amount of white marks, on chest, paws, jaws or skull, places a Yorkie into a tricolor classification and it is very wise to guard against this possibility.

The newly born Yorkie has a nose that is mostly gray, showing a small amount of pink on the edges of the nostrils. The nose should be a dark gray at around twenty-one days and definitely black by two months. It is very unusual to see a mismarked nose in a Yorkie and it should be considered a very bad problem.

The toenails are gray at birth, with an occasional white one. Any that fail to become black by two months are indicative of the availability of nonpigmented skin and hair.

The eye rims will be a dark red-brown birth, but should be black by two months. Very orangy red-gold tans will usually have lighter colored eye rims. This is not particularly desirable, but a sad fact of life. Unfortunately it also spoils the eye's expression.

Yorkshire Terrier puppies can be born with colors that automatically deprive them of the necessary qualities to become the proper colors of the breed. They can be born all black; all tan; tan with black

Tan changing and clearing on puppies at nine months (*left*) and five months. These puppies are owned by Jeanne Grimsby.

Clear tan face furnishings on Ch. Kelsbro Half Sovereign, owned by Lola S. Dowd.

Clear rich tans. Silverwind's Ode to Love (ten months), Ch. Wildweir Candytuft, Silverwind's Spirit of Apollo and Silverwind's Fantasia, all owned by Elissa Taddie.

133

points; tricolor: black, white and tan; all blue; bluish-gray with tan points, and so remain, or change to another shade of their newly born colors.

These mismarked Yorkie puppies are not the result of misalliances, or throwbacks but are rather the net product of incorrectly inherited genes, which have failed to activate the pigment glandular system to provide what is required to be in accord with the Yorkshire Terrier's breed Standard.

Puppies incorrectly colored or marked, should not be sold as "rare gold," "rare blue" or any other such gilded deceits. They should not be registered as Yorkshire Terriers, but should simply be found a loving home if one cannot bring oneself to have them put down.

The transition from newly born puppy to adult Yorkshire Terrier is a very confusing period. Any attempt by a novice to come to grips with this period by reading opinions of Yorkie breeders can only add perplexity to confusion. No one agrees. This fact alone offers the greatest hope to any breeder. The answer lies in the fact that a bloodline generally follows a course, but it never holds entirely true for all members of the bloodline.

Each Yorkie puppy commences its transition from the newly born black-and-tan to the adult blue-and-tan by its own inherited and constructed glandular system. The combination of its inherited genes from its sire and dam at conception, and the development of the fetus into a thriving newborn puppy, determines the health and makeup of the glandular system that supplies the pigment for the hair, skin, eyes, eye rims, nose and toenails.

The black, tan-pointed, newly born puppy must change into an adult with a pure clear golden tan and a pure even dark, steel-blue. Not all puppies achieve this goal. Some fail because their coat texture is unable to provide a means for light rays to be refracted and reflected to the human eye. Others fail because their systems fail to provide the necessary amount of pigment particles to the hair strands. Some fail because they inherit incorrect pattern placements. No matter what the cause, the result is that the Yorkie is unable to visually match the Standard in desired colors at specific areas.

To correctly match the Standard the Yorkie puppy must remove all black or blackish-brown hairs from its golden tan. This is first noticed on the skull which may go from black to tan at the hair roots, with any new outgrowth of hairs being tan. Or the hair on the skull

134

The litter brothers, Sorreldene Tangerine and Sorreldene Orange Boy—at seven months.

Eleven months later and the brothers have earned their championships, gotten a handle on their maturity and face bright futures.

may go from black to gray, with roots almost white, and any new outgrowth a very pale weak tan. In this last case, as the black intermingled hairs diminish the roots and new outgrowth will gradually assume a richer golden tan.

The black on the muzzle, sides of head, front ear base and around the eyes generally achieves a richer golden tan at the roots and new outgrowth as the black intermingled hairs diminish. These areas are always a darker shade of golden tan.

The chest and legs follow the same program as the skull. All early tan marks are always a richer tan.

In the case of a very light pale golden tan (creamy colored) there is usually no distinction between these early tan marks and the newly grown tan hairs.

The rear of the ear leathers are the last to surrender from the black's hold. They should be a deep rich warm golden tan minus any blackish hue. Failure of the ear to achieve a dark golden tan from the puppy black is very indicative of a Yorkie that will never clear its blue or clear its tan of black-hued hairs.

Most breeders in speaking of any Yorkie of any age, ask first about the tan. Puppies with early golden tan ears excite much envy.

The tan should never run out of its boundaries or this will give a fawn or bronzy appearance to the blue coat. This will be visible in a youngster at the shoulders, occiput and tail-set. Many a puppy reaching adulthood has slid past onlookers as having a broken blue when in reality it had a running tan.

The blue commences its transition from black to blue just above the hair roots and in the tips of the new-growing hairs. It may be visible first at the shoulder, loin, rump or the entire blue body, but it is visible on each and every hair in the area. It is not necessary to search through the coat. It can be easily seen by looking down onto the Yorkie which will be obviously acquiring a bluish cast to its coat.

Yorkies that have black coats as adults may often have diluted black-colored coats on the lower parts of their bodies, and digging into their coats will uncover this fact. However they are not blue but grayish-black and when looked down onto, they will never be bluish in cast.

The newly born to adult's skin pigment is identical in color transition as the outgrowing hairs.

The greatest block to a Yorkie's complete assumption of the desired colors is the failure of the coat texture. The newly born puppies

At eighteen months.

Two years, four months.

Three years, four months.

Four years.

How proper coat develops in the Yorkshire Terrier as seen in these studies of Ch. Wildweir Fair N' Square bred by Janet E. Bennett and Joan B. Gordon.

A veteran of ten years.

have flat, smooth coats. Only as the hair grows can texture be felt. It may be wiry, woolly, cottony or silky.

A wiry coat can develop the visually correct colors, but it will not attain great length. Most wiry coated Yorkies do change coat texture prior to one year. The hair at the roots commences to grow out a finer grade and thus becomes silky. Such puppies are, of course, an anathema to Terrier breeders, especially Scottish, Cairn and West Highland breeders.

The puppies with woolly and cottony coats, although growing great length and heaviness fast, never attain the correct visual colors. Their qualities—thick, heavy, downy and soft—deter or dull any light rays from proper play on the hairs.

Wavy coats are visible in Yorkie puppies at a very early age and in general portend a light silver adult. A slight waviness on the upper hindquarters is not unusual in many Yorkies, but should be watched.

"BREAKING" PATTERNS

As no two Yorkies ever seem to follow an extract transition pattern, or "breaking" as it has come to be termed, we have included the most general facts of this trying time:

A puppy that is about three to four weeks of age that shows gold hairs on the top of its head when the black hairs are parted, will as an adult have a clear golden tan. If the coat texture is silky, the blue will have no intermingled colors.

A puppy that has a wiry coat texture, with a tan that is a very bright red-gold by four to five months, will as an adult do one of two things: First, if the puppy as it approaches five or six months, or at least by nine months, shows the transition from black to blue, the coat texture will soften to a silky texture. If the black coat does not show this transition to blue, the adult dog will retain the wiry coat which will never attain any great length.

A puppy that has a bright orange-red tan by four or five months will as an adult have a bright steel-blue, which may have areas of lighter or darker blue. This coloring shows the greatest tendency to have the tan placements run into the allotted areas for the blue. The texture will be silky.

A puppy whose coat appears sparse or thin will, as an adult, have a thick, long coat of the correct fine silky, glossy texture. This coat's growth is like a human's hair, in that it is born with very little but by adulthood has an abundance of hair, the quantity having doubled and redoubled all during puppyhood (or childhood). Both colors will be totally clear.

A puppy of around four months, that has changed the color on its head from black to gray to a very pale cream color, will as an adult enrich all the tan areas to a clear golden tan. The blue will follow the correct manner of transition from black to blue starting to do so at around six months. The coat texture will be the correct silky type.

A puppy whose tan has been cleared of all the intermingled black or creamy hairs by four months and whose texture is fine and silky, will as an adult have correct colors. The tan of this puppy will probably enrich to a darker shade as an adult.

A puppy approaching adulthood with a thick, heavy coat that has pale cream-colored legs, sooty head colors, with intermingled black hairs in tan at the sides of the head and on the ears and ear fringes, may as an adult diminish some of these black and sooty hairs. Its desired blue area may eventually achieve a transition from black to gray but it will never have a clear golden tan, nor a dark steel-blue. The coat texture is either woolly or cottony.

A puppy approaching adulthood that has a black stripe in the center of its head, intermingled into the whiskers, the sides of the head and up into the topknot, with ears that are more visibly black than rich dark golden tan, will as an adult have a tan that is never totally cleared. As the years pass some of the black and sooty hairs will diminish, but a check of the pigment under these intermingled areas will show that it is a dark gray which will never lighten. The black on this dog will show a few hairs that will some years hence go from black to gray, especially at the lower hips and lower shoulders, when the hair is parted down through the upper layers. The coat texture will be woolly or cottony.

A puppy approaching adulthood that has intermingled sooty or black hairs at the sides of its head running up into the topknot, with a sooty area between the eyes, and whose ears are a sooty tan, will have a gray body coat by around three years. The gray will be lacking a blue hue. The tan will always have some intermingled sooty hairs especially at sides of the head, ear fringes and between the eyes. There may be some black or sooty hair on top of the muzzle but not in the foreface furnishings. The coat texture is cottony.

A puppy of three to four months that has a very pale gold tan and whose black has gone to light silver-blue, will as an adult be a light silver-blue. A check of this puppy's pigment will show that it is incorrect, as it will be light gray flesh color. The texture will be silky.

A puppy that shows coarse white hairs intermingled in the blue will usually shed most of these as it approaches adulthood.

A puppy approaching adulthood (or over a year) that has an inch-wide stripe from the hair root out, then blue, with the tip and last inch or two still showing its transition from black to blue, will with age lose the blackish tips on the end as they are worn off or cut off as the coat achieves floor length. The dark stripe will remain although it may lessen in width. It shows that the pigmentation of the hair is extremely dense at its beginning and does not diminish until it reaches this point. The tan will be clear, and the coat texture silky.

A puppy that at some stage in its puppyhood shows a brownish cast to its blue or black body coat is passing through a stage in which there is a hormone imbalance. This condition will normally right itself, as it is purely a growth stage.

All these are generalities and any puppy may follow a different path.

4. *How the Color Is Acquired*

What makes dogs have different colored coats of hair? Hair gets its color from pigment just like any other colored substance. Pigment is a coloring matter, either a powdered substance mixed with a suitable liquid, in which it is relatively insoluble, or any of various coloring matters in animals and plants.

Authorities believe that dogs have two major types of pigments. Dr. Clarence Little in *The Inheritance of Coat Color in Dogs* (Howell Book House, 1967) states:

> Like other laboratory mammals, dogs appear to have two major types of pigment in their coats. One of these is yellow, the other dark (brown or black). The color varieties of dogs have to be formed by various genes controlling the amount, extent and distribution of these pigments both individually, in combination or in competition with one another.
>
> Pigment granules can be distributed in various amounts and patterns in either or both the outside layer (cortex) or the inner portion (medulla) of the hair. Variations in such processes produce different optical color effects resulting in the different colors in different varieties of dogs.

A book on the study of horse color by Dr. Ben Green, *Color of Horses* (Northland Press, Flagstaff, Arizona, 1975), is interesting

Ch. Shadomountin Upper Cut, bred by Kathy Bucher and owned by Janet Jackson.
Don Petrulis

Ch. Trivar's Hell's Angel, bred and owned by Johnny Robinson and Morris Howard.

reading for anyone wishing to understand what makes the numerous individual hair colors.

Without resorting to complicated genetic terms, the process whereby hairs acquire colors and hues of that color are described. Though no similar study has been conducted on dogs, all mammals have the same system of hair coloration.

In horses there is only one pigment (melanin) and it is produced by glands situated in the hide of horses. The pigment, and the secretion it is suspended in, appear a brown color to the eye under a microscope. The pigment migrates into the hair shaft where it is arranged in varying patterns. The pigment granules, along with the refracted and reflected light rays directed from them, account for the visual multiple, different colors.

Hair is formed by the hair glands and may be divided into three parts. The *root*, situated in the inner skin layers, is flared. The *follicle*, above the root beneath the hair shaft, is a bulb-shaped cell containing a cavity. The *shaft* growing out of the follicle, consists of a clear outer wall and an inner core.

Pigment is secreted by glands in the inner skin layers and is picked up as the hair root moves in the layer. It is forced by its own electrons through the follicle and is forced out through the opening at the top of the follicle into the hair shaft. When the pigment granules force themselves through the follicle opening into the shaft, they form a pattern and migrate to the farthest outgrowth of the hair shaft in this pattern, unless there is an obstruction or diversion in the shaft.

The patterns are always the same for different hues of a color. They are thicker or thinner in the number, or size, of the granules making the pattern. The pigment in their patterns are deposited in many forms, perpendicular to the shaft, in geometric designs the length of the center of the shaft, in specific areas such as tip, along one inner wall, smeared against an inner wall, or in a circular formation inside the wall of the shaft with an open core, etc. The light rays are thus refracted, reflected, deflected, entirely or partially, and their courses redirected to the human eye.

Several shades of one color may show in varying areas in one animal, as a result of differing sizes or density in the pigment particles. More than one color pattern may overlap, creating a dual coloring.

Horses born black change colors because the hairs are situated in different skin layers. As the fine pigment glands in a layer cease to produce, the hairs are unpigmented, appearing white. Mingled with the black hairs the optically visual color is grayish, or mouse blue. The more unpigmented hairs mingled, the lighter the visual color will be until all skin layers cease producing sufficient pigment for the hair shaft, and the horse is whitish all over.

Sooty appearance derives when the tips are so constricted as to have a heavy concentration of pigment. Movement of the animal brings them together, giving the dirty blackish-brown smudged look.

In blue horses (Grulla), construction of the hair shaft is very complicated. It has a thin dense line of pigment granules which run the length of the center of the hair shaft. Stretching out from it to the walls are thin curtainlike partitions carrying pigment granules. This allows light to play directly on the inner line and the light is incompletely refracted from one wall of the shaft to the other, due to the partitions. The light is reflected back with a haziness which is perceived by the human eye as light blue or gray.

In golden-colored horses, such as the Palomino, the follicle is so constricted that the pigment granules flow through in a very fine line which is deposited as a smear on the inner wall of the shaft. Light rays penetrating through this smear are refracted and reflected in a glowing golden haze.

The people who wove the description of the Yorkshire Terrier into a breed Standard were very adept at animal husbandry. For nearly one hundred years their knowledge, which gained them advancement in the days of carriage trade, has stood to the advantage of the Yorkie in maintaining the breed's distinguishing points.

The new scientific understanding of color pigmentation of hair can be used to ensure us better Yorkies. It must be realized that we can no longer think only in terms of Mendelian genetics, where we have simple dominant and recessive effects governing the development of a trait.

We are dealing with multiple genes affecting the hairs' coloration. Each pair of genes (alleles) contribute to the desired trait. Each has a recessive and dominant form, but it is the number of gene pairs and their independent behavior from the other contributing genes during the process of recombination at fertilization that makes for the attainment of the Yorkies' desired prime important points of coat color and texture.

A Yorkie will not have a coat that is dense, long and straight, unless the hair glands produce many pliable, even hairs. Thick outer walls of the hair shaft impede the penetration of light. Rough, uneven surfaces of the outer walls deflect light rays.

The desired fine, silky texture gives the hair a thin outer wall that is strong and translucent. The hair is soft, clings to the body and feels cool to the touch. Woolly and cottony textured hairs have walls that dull the reflection of the pigment granules. The hair is rough, stands out from the body and feels warm to the touch.

A Yorkie minus the correct production (in extent, amount and distribution) of pigment granules can never achieve the desired lustrously glowing metallic colors of polished gold and steel-blue. The smooth surface of coat texture combined with the colors works in complete cooperation to produce the dog as visualized by Theo Marples in his first edition of *Show Dogs*:

"Beautiful to look at, active as a kitten, vivacious as the most 'Perky Pom,' the Yorkshire Terrier is the acme of Toy Dog virtue and perfection, looked at from every angle."

SIZE

From the beginning to the end of the AKC-approved Standard, you are informed that the Yorkshire Terrier is a small dog. In the beginning: "*Long-haired toy terrier*"—and at the end: "*Weight— Must not exceed seven pounds.*"

One is continually amazed to still read that it took many years and much crossing of breeds to bring the Yorkshire down to its Toy size. In the 1860s, they were shown in *"Toy Terriers—under five pounds."* By 1878, one top winner weighed in at ten pounds, and another top contender weighed four and three-quarter pounds. In 1891, weight was divided into two classes: "*under five pounds and over five pounds but not to exceed twelve.*" Came 1904 and weight had become three classes: "*five pounds and under,*" "*seven pounds and under but over five pounds,*" and "*seven pounds.*" One is not only amazed to read that it took many years to bring it down in size, but whoever passed judgment on what dogs fitted into *"seven pounds and under, but over five pounds"* has our congratulations.

It remains a fact that the animals that went into the production of the Yorkshire Terrier were small. Few exceeded twelve pounds in weight. It was never the question of the Yorkie being bred down in size. It is its cousins that have been bred *up* in size. Most of the early descriptions given of Skye and Scottish Terriers, etc., give weight at twelve to sixteen pounds.

When the Standard was rewritten in 1966, seven pounds was settled on. All the breeders and exhibitors belonging to The Yorkshire Terrier Club of America weighed their stock. The general agreement was that no one bred from animals over seven pounds. This weight would allow the larger bitches, who made the best brood bitches, to be shown without being penalized.

It was also settled that there would be no reference to sex. No one wished to penalize a male dog that carried the prime points that distinguish the breed—correct coat color and texture. Still, the desire was to keep the breed a small Toy dog. For this reason, the rule for weight simply specifies "*must not* exceed seven pounds."

8

Grooming

THE CARE that is given a Yorkshire Terrier's coat is all important. To keep a Yorkie groomed as a house dog is a fairly simple matter—a good brushing five minutes a day will do the job, with a bath given when needed, or desired. The topknot can be caught up in a wrap, ribbon, barrette or even cut short. But the care necessary for conditioning a show dog, and keeping it in show condition, is time-consuming and requires patience. It is a demanding job that allows no time off. Your one reward is that your Yorkie's perfection of a full floor-length mantle of gleaming gold and blue silken coat will reflect the amount of care it has been given.

The amount of coat that a Yorkshire grows depends on several things. First, the grooming must be done properly. Next, the dog must be healthy and happy. However, without the inherited ability to grow a long coat nothing is going to make the coat grow. If you wish a show dog then be sure that the dog you buy has the inheritance to grow a long coat.

Washing

Washing a Yorkie has improved some since the following description was written in 1893 in *Kennel Secrets* by "Ashmont." However,

147

because a lot of it is still timely it's included here. Obviously, since some of the same ideas for bathing have lasted this long, they must be important:

> While as a rule to wash a dog properly is not difficult, the washing of Yorkshire Terriers is an entirely different matter, and here the novice would be all at sea; in fact he should never attempt it on a good dog, for many a "crack" has been ruined in the tub; consequently for him should be given full directions.
>
> A foot pan is as good as anything to do the washing in. Place this on the table. Put in as much lukewarm water as will nearly reach to the dog's elbows. Mix in the soap until you have suds—never rub the soap on the dog. Now take a brush, a hairbrush that has a handle and long bristles, dip it in the suds and brush from the center of the back down, and always one way. The head must be washed in the same manner; brush from the center downward; in fact use the brush just as you do when not washing.
>
> When you are sure you have reached all parts and the hair and skin are thoroughly clean, pass the hand from the center of the back downward and force out as much of the soap and water as you can; then use the sponge in about the same way. This done, lift the dog out and put him into another tub, which is all ready on the table, containing clean lukewarm water, and brush him just as you did with the suds, until the soap is out. With the hands and sponge get out as much water as you can. Remove him from the tub and stand him on the table, put over him a cloth or towel and pass the hands over it with gentle pressure, that it may take up some of the water that remains in his coat; but on no account must the hair be rubbed or ruffled.
>
> Now after combing him with a comb that has widely-set teeth, begins a long and tedious process of drying. For this you must have two or three brushes; while one is being used, the others must be drying in front of the fire.
>
> This drying will occupy a full hour. When completed, take a little fine oil in the palm of the hand, rub the hands together and pass them over the coat. This done, tie up the "bang" with a piece of ribbon or tape to keep it from the eyes.
>
> Some dogs, in fact nearly all, will "fiddle"—scratch themselves— especially the very heavy-coated ones, which in hot weather may become heated and restless; and these must have "stockings" for the hind feet. The thumb of an old glove will fill the bill. Put the foot into this and tie with a piece of narrow tape around the leg.
>
> Let the dog run about in the room, provided you can watch him, for an hour or so. Then draw the brush over him a few times and "cage"

him. But do not oblige him to lie on plush, or velvet cushions, for they are far from suitable. A linen cover is the proper thing for a cushion, for it cannot stain nor does the coat adhere to it. And such a cover should be so made that it can be taken off and washed.

Even today, to prepare a Yorkie that has a full coat for a show takes time and, like growing coat, it cannot be rushed. If you don't have at least three or four hours to do your show dog's washing and grooming, don't start it. Granted, if the dog is not yet in full coat— i.e., floor length and wrapped—the length of time needed will vary per dog, but an hour at the least is needed for a young show prospect and probably more.

To wash a dog's coat for the show, you will need the following equipment:

Two hairbrushes
A comb
Toenail clippers
Scissors
Several large bath towels
A sponge or washrag
Shampoo—it should be one that is either manufactured for a dog's show coat or a regular shampoo for human hair.
A rinse—the rinse used will depend on the dog. For most Yorkies a cream rinse is best. However there are some dogs who have very oily coats and for these use a rinse made with vinegar and water, or a small amount of baking soda mixed with water.
A hair dryer.

Before washing the dog, the ears should be trimmed. The usual amount of hair to trim off is about one half, but this is an individual matter and has to be tried on each dog. If a dog has larger ears than are desirable, don't cut off so much hair that this becomes more apparent.

A few Yorkies have round tips. They shouldn't have, but not having read the part in the Standard that outlaws them, they still produce one or two that do. If your dog does have them, try and trim the hair to a point, rather than following the actual rounded tips.

Brush out all the dust, mats or snarls before you start. If the dog is wrapped naturally, remove the wraps and brush out the coat. If possible, brush the dog's coat out the day before and you'll save a little time. Once the dog is all brushed out, place the dog in the sink. Wet the coat thoroughly. If you have a spray attachment, it is a great help; otherwise you'll have to use the faucet and the sponge to get all the coat wet down to the skin. Shampoo the coat, but don't rub the hair round and round. A downward motion should be used. Be sure to wash the underside, and each leg should be shampooed separately including the pads and between the toes. To soap the long topknot, start at the scalp and work the shampoo from the scalp to the tip of the topknot. Don't rub it! Once you've shampooed all the coat and skin, rinse with lukewarm water until the hair has no soap left in it. Use the rinse and then, with your hand, press out as much water as you can by running your hands from the part downward. The whiskers and topknot—and the legs—can be gently squeezed between your fingers to remove the excess water.

Wrap the dog in a towel and pat out as much moisture as you can. It may be that you will need several towels to soak up the water. Once you've gotten as much out this way, place the dog on a dry towel and brush the coat dry in front of an electric dryer.

The coat should be brushed from the parting downward until every bit is completely dry. Be sure the legs and underside are dried completely before wrapping. A dog that is wrapped while damp will end up with a wavy coat when unwrapped. The long knot (*fall*) should be brushed dry by brushing the hair backward toward the tail.

Some dogs' coats look at their best right after a bath; others look better several days ahead of time, especially if they have coats that tend to be flyaway. For this reason it is best to determine on what day, after a bath, the dog's coat appears in best bloom, so that the dog can be washed that length of time prior to the show. Washing ahead of time will return some of the natural oil to the coat and make it more manageable. Very oily coats should be washed as close to show time as can be managed.

If you have any reason to feel that your dog has been in an area where it could acquire fleas, ticks or other bugs, be sure to use a good dip for them. One flea can cause enough damage to put a dog out of the show ring for months. No one has ever actually carried on experiments to measure how fast a coat grows, but we figure that about a half an inch a month is pretty close. (The blue coat usually tends to grow a bit faster than does the gold. Young dogs' coats grow faster, except when teething, than do the coats of more mature dogs.) If your Yorkie scratches a large hole you will have to wait until it is regrown, so it is easier to dip for undesirable guests than to wish you had. During the summer months it is wise to keep all the dogs dipped for fleas. Your veterinarian can recommend a good one; we have used Hilo dip for many years without any damage to the dogs' coats. It also usually helps to ward off any hot spots as well.

Oiling

If the coat is not being washed for a show, follow the above method for washing. If you are going to put the dog's coat in oil, you will find the fastest way is to use it as a final rinse. A pint of water with a teaspoon or so of oil poured over the dog will do the job nicely. One warning—use a separate brush for this process when drying your dog, and don't get it mixed up with your other brushes that you use for drying your dog for a show.

Be wary of using too much oil on a dog's coat, especially during the hot summer months, even if you do have air conditioning. Any dog whose coat is kept in oil should have the oil washed out regularly, as it tends to collect dirt and dust.

Wrapping

The questions of whether to wrap a show dog's coat, and at what age to begin wrapping, are the ones most often asked. No one has ever grown a full, floor-length coat on a male Yorkie without wraps, and only a very few bitches have ever achieved a full coat minus wraps. Even then the bitches usually had wraps on topknot, whiskers, tail and breeches. Wrapping is the only way to keep a coat from being soiled and the ends of the hair from being worn and broken off. The age at which to wrap the whole coat is usually around nine or ten months, sometimes later. The topknot should be done up as soon as it is long enough. The tail and breeches should be wrapped when they are getting long enough that wrapping will protect the hair from becoming constantly soiled. Hence the decision of at what age to wrap can only be made for each individual dog.

The other question invariably asked is how long does it take to get a Yorkshire into full coat once the coat is wrapped? It takes around two years to achieve the correct silky-textured Yorkie coat, although by around eighteen months you can usually begin to see appreciable results of your care. The woolly or cottony-coated dogs often have floor-length coats by a year, which is probably just as well for those who show this incorrect type, because if they had to wait longer, the dog's lack of correct color would be even more apparent. Again, time, patience and proper care are the best ingredients for achieving a full, floor-length coat.

To tie up the coat in wraps, use either waxed paper or Sav-a-Wrap midget size. This can be bought where bakery supplies are available. Other papers will do if they work for you. The paper or wrap doesn't grow the hair, it simply protects the ends from getting dirty or broken.

If a dog lives in a very warm tropical climate with high humidity, it has been found that either tulle or net is better for use as wraps as the hair needs the air circulation.

Brush the selected section of hair straight and wrap the paper around the hair like a tube. Double it over and put a rubber band around the folded paper, which can be folded either up or under toward the body. Use either medium-sized orthodontist bands or size eight rubber bands, available at stationery stores to secure the wraps. Make sure the roots of the hair are not being pulled too tightly or the dog will rub to loosen them. These wraps should be brushed out and redone every second day.

If a dog is just starting on being wrapped, it is best to start with the topknot, the tail, and the hair on either side of the tail, i.e., the breeches. In wrapping, anytime, be sure that the wraps do not impede the dog's movement. Sometimes Yorkies will ignore their wraps, even when wrapped for the first time; others will try to remove them. If this is a problem, a drop of Bitter Apple or Tabasco sauce on the wrap will usually put an end to any attempt at removal.

As to the number of wraps used, people vary on this—we have always used twenty-four wraps. Wrap the topknot in one, the chin whisker and each side whisker in one. The hair on the side of the head is parted from behind the ear and up to just before the eye. The side coat has five wraps, one on the neck, one on the shoulder, two between the front and rear legs, one on the hips. Each leg has a wrap, the chest, the tail and one on either side of the tail on the breeches. If you have a dog that scratches, it is best to put socks (boots) on the hind feet. Tube gauze works very well for this. You can usually buy it in a drugstore. The gauze for large fingers or toes—size two—is the best size. Cut a strip about six inches long, twist the strip in the middle then tuck one side into the other. Put the rear foot into the sock and

For the Yorkshire Terrier show dog, wraps are a fact of life. It is virtually impossible to cultivate a show coat without wrapping it to protect the dog's precious, silken tresses. This is Ch. Pride of Leyton, a son of Ch. Little Sir Model, owned by Catherine Miller, between shows.

When the wraps are removed and the full coat is prepared for an appearance in the show ring an amazing transformation takes place as the tiny dog in papers becomes a show dog without a peer. The model is Ch. Doodletown Tom Tom, bred by Vic and Lorraine Berry and owned by Janet E. Bennett and Joan B. Gordon.

153

wrap a narrow strip of tape around the top of the sock to keep it on, or use a piece of yarn or string. Don't wrap the tape too tight, and be sure the toes have room to move freely.

Trimming

For the show ring, and for any dog to really look its best, the overhanging hair on the feet and the hair between the pads should be trimmed. Since all dogs are extremely touchy about their feet, it's best to start trimming the paws while they are puppies. The toenails should also be kept cut back and they are easier cut right after a bath.

The paws should be trimmed as round as possible. Here again, study your dog; if the paws turn out too much, then trim the outside edge more than the inside edge—this will give the dog a better look. Shaggy-haired feet on a Yorkie detract from the dog's neat appearance and can make a dog appear to be moving incorrectly. The Standard specifies that feet be trimmed as round as possible.

When the coat of a Yorkshire becomes so long that it interferes with the dog's gait, it should be trimmed. A dog that is unable to move properly because it is stepping on its hair, or whose feet become entangled when gaiting, cannot present the proper picture. It's extremely foolish to assume that all a Yorkshire needs is a lot of hair. Most judges, in fact, approach a full coat with the idea that they are going to discover a fault hidden beneath the dog's flowing tresses. They expect, and rightfully so, that the dog can and will move proudly around the ring with the other dogs who may have less coat, so don't put your dog at a disadvantage by allowing his coat to become so long that it detracts. If the coat is too long, cut it. Most Yorkies, if they are carrying an excessive length of coat, look out of balance—an extralong trailing coat can make a dog appear to be long bodied.

To trim an overly long coat, first brush the dog all the way out, removing all the wave. Be sure the dog is not standing on any of its coat. The dog should be standing close to the edge of the table so that the coat can be brushed straight down over the edge.

When the dog gaits, the hair will tend to spring up a bit; you should trim the side coat from the rear leg forward, so that there is between an inch to an inch and a half hanging over the edge. From the rear leg backward, trim it slightly longer like the train of a dress. Across the chest and in front of the front legs leave plenty of clearance so that the dog's gait can be seen—one half inch over the edge is usually about right. All this trimming should be done slowly and carefully. Try cutting a little and then gaiting your dog until you find the length that allows the dog a free and easy gait. If the whiskers are so long that the dog walks on them, they should be trimmed as well.

Trimming a Yorkie in full-show coat should be done by someone who knows what they are doing, never by someone who has never done work with a Yorkie's coat. Trimming a show coat is always scary as one is always sure that you're cutting too much—but even if one were to end up floor length, better that, and a dog that can gait properly, than one that cannot because its coat is too long.

Brushing

All Yorkshires need to be brushed and no show coat was ever attained without proper application of the brush. The brush should be made with pure bristles, and they should be of variegated lengths, not too soft but rather stiff. Don't use a nylon bristle or pin brush, for the hair ends will be split and the coat growth will be retarded.

It is best to either dampen the brush, or spray the coat lightly with water or a coat dressing, of which there are a number made for dogs. The hair should be brushed from the part downward. Some people prefer to brush the dog by laying the dog in their lap; however, we prefer to brush the dog while the dog is standing. Be sure to brush all the coat and to leave no snarls or tangles anywhere. A comb is used to put a part in the dog; it is not used to pull out snarls. Most important in good grooming is patience and gentleness—don't ever get mad at the dog during a grooming session.

Brushing out a Yorkie to get it ready for the judging at a show follows much the same process as brushing out the dog's coat at any other time. All wraps are removed. They can be all removed at one time and the whole coat brushed, or each undone separately and the coat in it thoroughly brushed out. Any wave should be brushed out so that the coat lies flat and straight and the coat should be brushed until it shines. The coat will achieve a natural shine almost immediately, that is assuming that bathing and coat conditioning have been done properly. Woolly or cottony coats never have the proper natural shine that makes the hair look like silk-satin, and when in motion "like running water." The parting down the center of the dog's back should be made as straight as you can make it.

The grooming requirements of the Yorkshire Terrier are admittedly demanding and call for deep commitment on the part of those who seek success in the show ring. The rewards, however, in satisfaction and achievement justify the hard work fanciers are called upon to deal with. The model is Irish and Am. Ch. Gleno Playboy, bred by Eugene Weir. *Glenview Studio*

The Ribbons

To put on the dog's ribbon take down the topknot and brush it out completely. Then make a part from the corner of the dog's eye to halfway or center of the dog's head, making a V-shaped part—the point of the V facing toward the rear of the head. Place a rubber band— a medium or small-sized orthodontist band—at the base of the hair of the topknot. Take the underneath ends of the topknot and gently pull them backward. Then separate these hairs, taking a few hairs in the center. Hold these hairs and slide the rubber band forward so the front hair is loosened and softens the dog's expression. Do not make this hair into a pouf as you do not want a round head on a Yorkie and an overlarge pouf detracts from the dog's appearance.

The orthodontist bands can be purchased from a dog grooming equipment supplier or at a dog show. They are available in various colors or clear: most exhibitors use the medium-sized bands.

Next comes the ribbon. Most exhibitors use readymade bows with the rubber bands already attached. Again, these are available where the rubber bands are sold. It is best to have an exhibitor show you how to make the bows from scratch. If you prefer to tie your own bows on—you need ribbon that is an inch wide.

Picking the color for the dog's ribbon is a matter of personal preference. As a general rule, however, pastel colors, black, brown, yellow and white tend to fade the dog's color and do not stand out well in the show ring. Bright colors are best. Young dogs whose golds are not completely cleared tend to look best with red or orange ribbon as it picks up the gold minimizing the black or sooty spots.

Fold the topknot over so you have a small knob standing up. Holding the ribbon by its rubber band, place the ribbon over the knob so it faces backward. Bring the ribbon back over the knob so the ribbon is placed facing forward. The hair behind the top knot and in front of the ears is parted in the center and brushed down either side in front of the ears. How much hair is drawn into the topknot or left out depends on the thickness of your dog's topknot. Trial and error is the only way to be sure you have it right, so practice at home till you know what looks best before the day of the show.

Two ribbons are allowed by the Standard, but this style is rarely used, one bow being preferred.

If your Yorkie has long whiskers you may want to place them in a barrette or catch them up to keep them from getting dirty or wet before going into the ring.

Over a period of time certain grooming fads and practices come into a breed. Some become so commonplace that as each new generation of exhibitors enters a breed they see them being done and accept them as correct or allowable grooming procedures.

However, it must be realized that some of these procedures were started to disguise a fault on a particular dog being groomed.

For example, improper head structure or expression may be artfully camouflaged when the topknot is teased and tied into a large pouf or puff.

Trimming, thinning or sculpting a dog's coat is done for a number of reasons, all to disguise a structural fault by camouflaging it optically with these above procedures.

Artificially coloring the dog's blue or gold to improve the color is illegal and should never be done.

Tying the dog's ear fringe into its topknot to improve the ear carriage is yet another objectionable practice.

None of these disguises will fool an expert judge, since they are optical illusions. An alert judge will realize the artifice as soon as he or she starts to examine the dog.

Every exhibitor who uses these practices has made a choice to be a designer rather than a breeder. True breeders are well aware that the only way to remove undesirable traits is to breed them out. No other way is acceptable to them, nor should be to any dog person.

Grooming the Brood Bitch

A brood bitch can be kept in show coat if she is to be returning to the ring, but it takes patience and common sense. If the bitch's coat is wrapped, it will have to be brushed every day, a little at a time, as the puppies cannot be without their mother for long periods. If the show coat is not wrapped, keep it lightly oiled with a pure oil and brush it twice a day. It is best to wrap the hair on the tail and the breeches—the hair on either side of the tail—to keep it clean. If this area gets dirty, rinse it off, dry it, brush it out and rewrap. For a brood bitch that is not being kept in a show coat, a light brushing every day is best, or the coat can be trimmed down before the bitch whelps her puppies. Once you start giving the puppies a meal, usually at around three weeks, the bitch can have a bath, but don't use anything but a pure shampoo and light pure oil rinse. Some bitches do shed a little of their coats, but if they are brushed regularly it stays nominal.

Grooming the Puppy

The first grooming that a Yorkshire Terrier puppy gets is when the puppy's ears, paws and toenails are trimmed for the first time.

Puppies need their ears trimmed as soon as it is apparent the hair is overhanging the edges of the ears. The weight of too much hair on a puppy's ear can cause the ear to hang down, rather than remain erect or come up properly. This is usually visible around three weeks of age if the coat is extremely heavy. Very heavy hair on a puppy's ear is usually a pretty good indication that the texture is going to be either woolly or cottony. Silky-textured coated puppies do not have as heavy a growth of hair on their ears. The hair should be trimmed as far down on the edges, back and front of the puppy's ear as soon as possible, if the hair is very heavy. On puppies with silky-textured coats, the hair should be trimmed three quarters of the way down, which is further than it will be trimmed as the puppy grows.

The scissors that are used should be sharp and have a blunt point. These can be purchased at a drugstore or sometimes from pet suppliers. In drugstores they are usually sold for babies. Trimming a puppy's ear takes extreme care and lots of patience. They are usually wiggling around and interfering in any way that they can. Hold the puppy in your lap, take the ear gently, but firmly, with your fingers. Feel the edge of the ear with your fingers and trim along the edge carefully. To remove the hair from the back and front, roll the leather of the ear over your fingers—the hair stands up and it is easier to trim. If you have trouble finding the ear's edge, dampen the ear and the edge is more visible. Whatever happens, treat the puppy gently and encourage it; don't frighten it by fighting with it over its wiggling. If you have to change from ear to ear, as the puppy insists on turning around, do so. If it does not get scared, it'll settle down and let you get on with the job—at least for a couple of minutes. Once the puppy realizes that it is not being hurt, you'll find that the trimming can be done quickly with a minimum of twists and turns.

The paws are trimmed by gently trimming the overhanging hair from around the paws and between the pads. Dogs are very touchy about their feet, so be careful. It may also be advisable to trim the hair under the tail to prevent the puppy from getting soiled.

Toenails usually need to be trimmed before anything else, and should be done as soon as they appear to be scratching their mother when they nurse. This can be anywhere from ten days to three weeks. Toenails that are left too long can be very uncomfortable for the mother, and long nails can catch in the bedding, causing a puppy to dislocate or strain a leg while trying to get the toenail free.

Bathing the Puppy

Since the coat of a Yorkie demands a clean, healthy skin to grow, we usually start washing our puppies at around two months of age. The first bath should be given at a time when the puppies are their most active. Don't pick a time when they are worn out from playing and are usually napping. Don't wash a puppy if it has had an upset stomach, been ill, doesn't act just right, or had shots that day. If you have friends coming to see the puppies, wash the puppies the day before, not the day they come. Too much excitement in one day can bring on an upset. If the puppy is going to a new home, the bath should be a day ahead. The puppy is not going to get that soiled in twenty-four hours. If the puppy does get a little soiled, a damp washrag should do the job of cleaning it up.

For the puppy's first bath, support the puppy in your hand or with only its rear feet touching the bottom of the sink. Using a sponge or washrag, wet the puppy thoroughly; if the puppy wants to look at the sponge, the running water or sink—let it—but don't let it get scared by slipping or getting water in its mouth or eyes. If the puppy isn't frightened while being washed now, or at any later time, the whole job will be a lot easier for both of you. Having gotten the puppy wet, apply shampoo and gently wash it all over. Care should be taken around the face, but do wash it as well, including the ear leathers. Using the sponge, or washrag, rinse it thoroughly getting out every bit of soap. Wrap the puppy in a large towel and rub the coat dry. It is only for the first couple of baths that rubbing the coat dry is advisable; after that, too much damage is done by rubbing. Once the puppy is dried as well as possible, take another dry towel and, with the puppy in your lap, use a hair dryer and brush the coat to finish getting it all the way dry. After the puppy's bath, plenty of time should be allowed for a long nap before the puppies have any more excitement.

From this point on the puppies should be washed every two weeks until they are around five months, after which time we usually wash them once a week. Of course, if the dog is a house pet and its coat is not being grown for show, a bath can be given less frequently. No puppy should be allowed out-of-doors until at least several hours have elapsed from when it was bathed. And no puppy or dog should ever be washed if it is not feeling well.

Puppies should start being brushed early, but the hairbrush should not be as firm as the one used on the coat of an older puppy. Brushing should be done daily.

Grooming the Pet Yorkshire

The care of the nonshow coat of a Yorkie should be much the same as of a dog being conditioned for the show ring. Both need to be brushed regularly, kept in good health and kept clean. A few minutes of brushing every day will keep the dog looking like a Yorkie should and it is really only fair to the dog. Unfortunately for the pet dog, the best of intentions sometimes deteriorate and the brushing is left undone—until one day the owner realizes what a snarled mess the dog's coat has become. At this point they are usually at a loss as to how to undo the damage, and are too ashamed to call the breeder. Often it becomes an ordeal for the dog and owner as the owner tries to comb out the snarls. Here, then, are a few ways that help make it easier on everyone:

First off, don't try to comb out the coat. Snarls should be undone while the coat is damp. Give the dog a bath and rinse with a rinse made of bath oil (or any oil) mixed with water. Squeeze the excess water out of the dog's coat, then start brushing. When you come to a snarl, separate it with your fingers, using the brush to help break up the mats. Hold the snarl so that your fingers are above the snarl and against the skin—this way the pull is against your fingers rather than pulling against the dog's skin. The very woolly-type of coat usually mats, and if the mat is too tight it is best to cut these out if the brush and fingers cannot separate them. On the cottony-type coat, the snarls are close to the skin and present the hardest problem to undo. If—after washing and brushing—any mats remain, and with this type coat they probably will, they will have to be cut out. Being so close to the skin, too much brushing will irritate the skin causing sores. The cut places, or even if the whole coat is cut, will regrow just as human hair does. A dog with the correct silky-type coat can get snarled due to lack of

If the calendar and the climate permit, a senior citizen can be very happy in a cut-down coat.

A pet Yorkshire or a retired show dog can be made to look very attractive in a modified Schnauzer trim. This retains terrier character but does not require the work needed by a full show coat.

Maintaining a full show coat on an older dog is an option some owners do select. This is Wildweir Forget-Me-Not, owned by Vic and Lorraine Berry, at age nine in a glorious covering that still maintains its vigor.

care, but they never snarl as badly as do the other type coats. A bath given as above, with a good brushing, will generally remove any snarls leaving a silky-coated Yorkie silky-coated again.

An elderly dog should be brushed regularly, but should not be washed as often as younger dogs, and only when the dog's health is good. An older dog's circulation is not what it was when it was younger, so keep a check on the skin for any sores, and don't overtire the dog by brushing it too long at one time. If you can't keep an older dog brushed, then the coat should be trimmed short.

The time and care put into your Yorkie, whether a pet or a show dog, will be repaid. Its coat will not shed out so all your work will last as long as its care is maintained. Long or short, its gleaming silky tresses, tossed about in play or parade, will be your eye-filling reward.

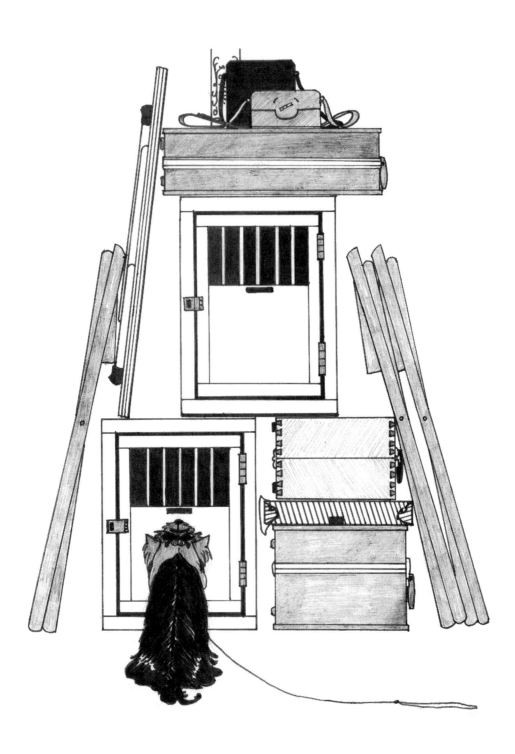

9

Showing Your
Yorkshire

THE SHOWING of Yorkshire Terriers can be fun for the whole family or a hobby for a single individual. Yorkies adapt well to competition in obedience, conformation or junior showmanship—and it is not unusual for one Yorkie to participate in all three, being shown by a different family member in each.

If you have never shown before, we suggest that a first step would be to attend a dog show in your area (without your dog) and see what it entails. If you can, contact a local Yorkshire Terrier or all-breed club (your veterinarian may be able to steer you to one) for guidance. Otherwise, an inquiry to the American Kennel Club, 51 Madison Avenue, New York, N.Y. 10010, will bring you answers on shows in your area, where to contact clubs, or on the requirements for showing.

To enter your Yorkie at a show, it must be at least six months of age, and registered with the AKC. Assuming that you will look to local clubs or the AKC for information on the classes to enter, or how a dog earns points toward championship, we will confine ourselves here to pointers that may be of help in actually showing your Yorkshire.

It is the exhibitor's job to help make the best of his dog. The dog show ring is not the place to start training your show dog. Teach your dog to walk properly, to stand still on the table and ground, and to be examined by different people. A few seconds spent on the following things, while your puppy is under three months, will help assure that they will not be stumbling blocks in its show future:

1. Put the puppy on a table, keeping your hand close by it so that it knows you are close. The first couple of times on a table, the puppy may lie flat down and just look around. Next, it will slowly stand up and take a few sniffs around. A tidbit fed on the table will help. The puppy has to get the idea that it is safe up there. Just think how you'd feel if someone put you way up on something twenty feet off the floor. Some puppies are never bothered and will start off all over the table, so keep a hand near the puppy.
2. Try using a word such as "up" or "table" when you lift your puppy up to place it on the table. In this way it will be ready; otherwise that lift up can have the same effect as a fast elevator ride.
3. Don't put the puppy, or allow it to be put, on a table when being given an inoculation.
4. Once the puppy appears to accept the table and height—then start teaching it to stand.
5. Teaching the puppies to follow your feet will make leash breaking easier for everyone.

Shows are held both outdoors and indoors, so your Yorkie should be trained to walk on grass as well as on cement, dirt and rugs. Grass at most outdoor shows is anything but ideal for Toy dogs. It does help if you have prepared your Yorkie for such a circumstance. One way to do this is to first walk it in grass that is overdue to be mowed, and then walking it through mowed grass in which the clippings have not yet been picked up.

No Yorkie should be shown if it is not in condition. A Yorkie that is too fat, too thin, has a scratched-out coat, is not bathed, or is simply under the weather, hasn't got a chance of winning. A Yorkie that is not lead broken, that won't stand for the judge to examine, or that is simply scared due to not having been accustomed to strange surroundings, is not going to win. No matter how much coat, or how perfect its color, if the judge cannot see your Yorkie walking proudly, or examine it to feel its construction, or look at its teeth, he is not going to place the dog. A show dog is just that—a dog that shows itself so that the best points can be seen.

Remember that in entering your dog at a show, you are actually asking for a judge's opinion of it. Be honest with yourself in evaluating your dog against the standard. Realize that while a young dog may have a great future, if it meets up with a mature dog that is in its prime, youth will generally have to give way. Judges are required to judge the dogs as they appear on the day they are shown—not on their futures or pasts. And if you lose, but don't feel you should have, don't get upset—seek other judges' opinions at other shows.

At the Show

A lot of worry about that first show can be eliminated by knowing where, what and when. If the show is unbenched, the time to arrive depends on how many Yorkies you have to get ready. A good average is one half hour for the grooming of each dog. Then allow time to get your Yorkie exercised, your equipment set up and a look around. If you have never shown under the judge, find where your ring is located. It is best to locate its position anyway. Trying to find it at the last minute will only upset you and your exhibit. Having found the right ring, watch how the judge manages the ring—in other words, does he gait the dogs up and down the mat, in a triangle, or in an ''L'' pattern? Are the dogs examined on the table and then gaited, or does he examine each dog before gaiting the dogs?

If you are the first breed in the ring at the specified hour, check to see if the judge is running on time or not. If there are other breeds listed before Yorkies at the specified hour, then you have to guess as to what time it will be. But since you came to show your Yorkie, it is better to be too early at ringside than too late. Take your crate to the ringside. At some shows you cannot bring your crate to the ringside; if this is the case, bring a large towel to the ringside and spread it out on the floor for you and your Yorkie. If the dog is young, allow time for it to look around and see where it is while it sits in your lap or you hold it in your arms. Put it down by your feet, after being sure there is room and that there are no large dogs or children in strollers too close, and let it study the whole place from its angle—which is naturally a much lower view than we humans ever see at a show. Then get it groomed up.

Ask the ring steward for your armband and put it on your left arm with number visible to the judge.

Learning all the ways to make the best of your Yorkie's good points and minimize its faults is best learned by watching other people show their dogs. Trial and error is very good experience. Getting a friend to come and watch you show your Yorkie so that he can tell you where you made mistakes is always a big help.

One question that invariably arises is whether to show your own dog or hire a handler. Frankly, our opinion is that any owner is as capable as a handler of doing a good job with their Yorkie so long as the owner tries. It is the owner's job to get the Yorkie into the proper show condition. An owner who is willing to learn to groom a Yorkie for the ring usually can spend more time doing it than can a handler who has a number of breeds to show.

It takes a few shows for a novice and young dog to work well together, but if an owner has the desire he can learn. A lot of people seem to feel that they cannot win unless they have a handler. This fallacy is given credence when a beginner, having failed to win with his Yorkie, hires a handler to show his dog and the dog wins. The owner immediately supports the supposition that judges only look at handlers, forgetting the obvious—that he, the owner, was making no effort to learn how to show his Yorkie, whereas the handler he hired made every effort to present and show the Yorkie to its best advantage. The second argument put forth is that handlers are the backbone of dog show because they are professionals. Frankly, if there were no breeders, there would be no dog shows—hence, no necessity for handlers. If a person is physically or emotionally unable to show their Yorkie then, obviously, a handler is necessary. Again, sometimes, for various reasons, an owner cannot get away from home and then must employ a handler. Of the sixty-eight Yorkies that have won Best in Show, forty-eight have been shown by their owners.

A question usually asked by those attending their first show with their new show prospect is "What do I need to take with me?" If one were to be absolutely technical, "The dog and a leash" would be the answer, but there are things that make the job easier. So, starting with your dog, here is a list of suggestions:

1. A crate. Actually with a Yorkie this is something that is best to purchase early in your Yorkie's life. When driving in a car, it gives your dog the same kind of protection your seat-

belt affords, should you stop suddenly. If your dog is crated when you have to go into a restaurant, or stop where you cannot take the dog with you, windows can be left open for air without its getting out or someone reaching in to steal your dog. At shows, your Yorkie will appreciate the quiet security of its own place. The crate, be it a wire one, wood or whatever, should be large enough for your Yorkie to lie, stand or sit. A crate eighteen inches long is ideal. For summer, it should be open on three sides at least; and— if it is a wire crate—for winter it should have a cover, or sides that have air holes in them. There are crates made that have removable sides for the summer, which re-inserted provide winter comfort for your dog. The wire crates have canvas covers you can buy, or you can make one yourself.

2. A pad, towel or rug to sleep on in its crate, or for its bench, if it is a benched dog show.

3. A padlock—for the crate, or benching, in case you have to leave it alone for a short time.

4. A chain on which to put the padlock, when locking your benching at a benched show. A big chain collar is fine for the job.

5. Grooming equipment for your Yorkie.

6. Water. It is best to bring water from home for your dog. A change can upset it and put it off its best performance.

7. A water bowl.

8. Extra towels.

9. A folding chair or chairs. Although some buildings provide these, it's easier to be sure you have a place to sit.

10. A table. A grooming table can be purchased at most shows, or you can use a TV table or card table.

11. Some kind of tidbit that your dog enjoys so you can bait it to get its attention in the ring.

12. You'll find paper towels, Kleenex or some kind of wipes a good idea to have along.

There are other pieces of equipment that are useful, but until an owner is showing more than one dog, they just aren't necessary. These include a wire pen in which to exercise your Yorkie and wheels to transport your equipment from the car to the building.

What the Judge Is Looking For

If this is your first time in the show ring, it's kind of handy to have an idea of what the judge is looking for—that is, what the judge is doing in the course of making his (or her) decision.

First, if your dog isn't trained, you've handicapped yourself and given the judge his number one reason for not placing your dog. Do follow the directions on training your dog. In that way the judge will be able to determine that your Yorkie is the most perfect animal in the ring—just as you are sure it is.

Second, the name of the game is to determine your "perfect" Yorkie's faults and try to make them less obvious.

The judge first assembles all class entrants in a line, and checks exhibitors' armbands to be sure that all are present and that no one from another class is in the ring. The judge may study the dogs in their lineup or he may gait them around the ring. In this, he is trying to get a general impression of how well each dog's body is proportioned, and of the overall balance of the dog. Next, he wants to see the dog's topline, which should be level, the same height at rump as at the shoulders.

You have two possible problems here. If your Yorkie has not been in a group of other Yorkies its attention may stray to the animals in front, or behind. This will not help its topline, for it will be off-stride. Try getting its attention back on you. A tasty tidbit, small enough so that it does not have to halt while it chews it up, will help; even a whiff of it will recall it to you.

The other problem is that it may decide it'd rather judge the spectators hanging over the ringside. If it's the first show let it have a look; after all, you'd let it study things in a new room. You may give the judge a score here, but you'll gain a step at your next show.

Try keeping your Yorkie's head up—to prevent it from acting like a scent hound. When it investigates the entrancing odors of the well-used matting, its head and neck go down, it goes off-stride and to compensate, its backbone angles down, unleveling its topline.

If the weather is cold, or your Yorkie is nervous about the whole procedure, it'll probably roach its back. You can only hope that, given time, it'll level it out. Of course, if it isn't level when your Yorkie is safely home and "Lord" of all it surveys, it isn't going to level out at the show and the score goes against you.

The judge, after gaiting the dogs around, motions the owners to

Steadiness on the table is essential for every Yorkshire Terrier show dog. Careful conditioning from early puppyhood is necessary for this.

All dogs, regardless of size, must be able to present a flattering picture on the ground. A Yorkshire should reflect self-confidence at all times and never back away from a judge who knows how to act around Toys.

halt, and has the first Yorkie in line placed on the table for examination. Sometimes the judge wants the dog placed on the table a certain way, so pay attention to the judge as well as your dog. In fact, pay attention to the judge at anytime he or she is giving instructions. The judge will appreciate the courtesy, and you'll score points in gamesmanship.

Set your dog up. The front legs should not turn out at the elbow, but stay close to the chest. You want them far enough apart to give the appearance of its having a compact, square body, not a shelly body. Place the rear legs so that the hocks are straight down and parallel to each other, but apart. The legs should have a slight bend at the stifle. Now pray that your Yorkie stays that way while you tidy up its coat.

Hold it by its leash in front and a hand close to the tail. Please don't try the "Look Mom, no hands!" bit; you can never be sure that the table isn't going to collapse, or that some distraction will not materialize. You don't want to pick up a Yorkie with a broken leg, while you explain that the animal never jumped, or fell off, the table before. Besides, your touch on the dog gives it confidence.

The judge then examines the Yorkie. There are generally two ways of doing this. First, the judge will get the dog's attention to check its expression. A nice, dark, sparkling eye, framed by dark eye rims, is a point-getter here. Small V-shaped ears, well set up on the skull, and used—when interested—help your Yorkie (along with its eyes) display a sharp, intelligent expression. Ears tied up into the topknot are easily caught by any judge. If your dog's are low-set, you'll just have to hope that the ears of the other exhibits are also, or that your Yorkie is so much better elsewhere that you won't lose more than a slivered point here. The judge looks to be sure the nose is black; that the head, viewed from the side, is a rather flat line, not a deep stop; that the muzzle is not too long and that the skull is not round (apple-headed). The judge then checks the bite (teeth).

An alternative procedure is for the judge to first check the dog's bite (teeth) to see if it is scissor or level. Either way, here's where you cross your fingers. A Yorkie's head isn't all that big and a human hand can encompass at least two thirds of it. Hopefully, the judge will not cover your Yorkies' eyes while checking the bite. Yorkies, like most animals, prefer to see what anyone is doing in their mouths and, if they can't, they back away and all your careful leg arrangement is thrown into disarray. If this happens, don't glower at the judge, just try a fast move to get them rearranged. Judges make "brownie" points with exhibitors when they ask the exhibitor to show them the dog's bite, and it's a lot more healthy as judges do not have time to wash their hands between examining each dog. However, the judge is Captain of the Ring and you do what he or she asks.

The judge looks at the tan headfall for color—a rich, golden tan, distribution and purity from intermingled black hairs. He checks to see if it is deeper in color at the sides of the head, at ear roots, on the muzzle, with the ears a deep rich tan. He checks that the tan does not extend down on the back of the neck.

The judge checks that the chest hairs are a bright, rich tan. The forelegs are checked to be sure they have black toenails and that the bright, rich tan does not overreach itself and grab a piece of the blue's territory. The judge also looks for any stray black or gray hairs in the forelegs' tan.

The judge checks the hindlegs to be sure that the tan doesn't extend higher than the stifle. He checks the rear legs for construction and the tail set (placement). If it is a male dog, he checks to be sure the Yorkie has two testicles of even size and that they are properly descended.

Then the judge studies the Yorkie's body to be sure that it is compact, all portions properly balanced to give an overall well-proportioned stamp. He checks to be sure the backline, viewed from the side, is level and that it is the same height at the shoulder as at the rump; that the chest is broad enough for plenty of heart room and lung expansion, and that the loin is short and broad so that there is enough room for all the body's internal organs. He checks that the hip joints are correctly formed.

Then the outer covering of the body, its hair, is checked. The steel-blue is to extend up the neck to the base of the skull and not into the tan on the skull. The blue covers over the body, onto the tail which is checked to be sure that it is a darker shade of blue and even darker at the tip. The blue is looked at to be sure that it is a pure blue minus any fawn, bronzy or black hairs in the blue. You, as the exhibitor, can only contribute to your gains here by presenting a healthy, well-conditioned Yorkie in muscle and flesh—your Yorkie's coat clean and thoroughly groomed.

The last thing, or the first thing—depending on the judge—is whether the coat texture is glossy—whether it shines. The hairs are each fine and silky. The quality of this point will be determined by your dog's inheritance and your conditioning.

The judge, having examined your Yorkie, will ask you to move

The lessons of lead training and showing on the floor will prove themselves well worth the time and effort when puppies compete against each other in Sweepstakes, Specialties and other important shows.

A PROUD MOMENT FOR A BREEDER—*Kennel Review* conducts an annual "Tournament of Champions" that honors many achievements in the dog fancy. In 1985 the Wildweir ladies were honored as the Top Toy Breeders in the United States. At the presentation (from *left*) Janet Bennett handled Ch. Wildweir Storm Warning, Joan Gordon had Ch. Wildweir Doorprize and Nancy Donovan showed Ch. Wildweir's Wicked Countess. The judges were J. Fred Peddie, Michelle Billings and Peggy Westphal. *Missy Yuhl*

your exhibit so he can evaluate the dog's gait. Leash training pays off in your dog's ability to step along beside you confidently on a loose leash. Each judge has his own pattern for observing movement. Do it the way the judge instructs. If you don't hear or understand the directions, ask for clarification. You may improve your chances here by calling your Yorkie's name before you execute a turn. Your dog will then be forewarned of a change in gaiting or direction.

Most judges halt the dog as it returns to them. Let your dog know it is about to come to a halt. Having gotten its attention, your Yorkie will halt for you in an alert manner.

The judge will indicate where he wishes you to place your dog; if he doesn't want you to, return to the end of the line. Tidy up your Yorkie's coat. Tell your dog what a great creature it is. Make your Yorkie feel everybody is having a great time. This will inspire you also.

Now if at this point your Yorkie decides to move around, sit down or climb in your lap, take comfort in that you are not the first to experience this nor will you be the last. A young dog should enjoy its first shows and a few goofs won't hurt; there will be many other shows, but not if your show prospect gets frightened or upset at the start of its career. It can feel your emotions, so relax. A Yorkie that has a good time at the beginning will end up being an easy dog to show.

Move your exhibit along as the lineup moves forward. As the judge is gaiting the last dog in the line, arrange the coat and legs of your Yorkie. Get its attention, but let it stare at the judge if it wishes; it may catch the judge's eye and hook a few more points for you. The judge now finishes the evaluation of the exhibits and places them.

Should your dog win its class, you must return to the ring with the other first-prize winners of your dog's sex when Winners class is called. If you get second, stay at the ringside because should the dog that beat you get Winners, you will have to go back in the ring to compete for Reserve Winners. If you are lucky enough to take Winners, you go back into the ring when the competition for Best of Breed is called. Should you be in doubt, ask an experienced exhibitor; oddly enough every exhibitor did have a first show with just as many fears and qualms, even though some tend to forget this fact.

Can. OTCH Heskethane Sixpenny Bit, UD, owned by Carole Klein, tries on the trophy for size that she won as High in Trial against all breeds at the Queensboro KC show in 1991. "Penny" bowled the judges over again that same year at the Gaines regional Super Dog competition and earned the award for Highest Placing Toy Dog.

10

Obedience Training and the Yorkshire Terrier

By Shirley Patterson

ONE DAY while Marjorie Davis of Boca Raton, Florida, was preparing her eight-year-old Yorkie, Smokey, for a training session on her front lawn, disaster came frighteningly close. Smokey spied another dog across the street. Without further thought, he darted toward the dog. Marjorie saw the oncoming car and shouted at the top of her lungs, "Down!" Her dog dropped, the car passed, and Marjorie drew a sigh of relief. Obedience training had saved her beloved Smokey.

Practical Applications

As this example demonstrates, obedience is a vital part of any dog's life. But training can be used not only to save your Yorkie's life; it also can help to make life a lot simpler for you, as I once discovered. My Yorkies liked to play a game of hide and seek in the covers every morning when I tried making my bed. One day the thought occurred to me to put my dogs' obedience skills to work. I sat my Yorkies on the floor with a sit-stay command and cut bed-making time in half.

Marjorie Davis uses the same command when she takes several dogs to the veterinarian's office. Each dog is placed on a sit-stay on a bench in the waiting room, until it's its turn to be examined. This exercise can also be used when you open your front door or when friends are visiting. Let's face it, not all people are dog lovers. Some do not enjoy being sniffed, licked and jumped upon, especially if they are wearing their best clothes.

From the moment you take possession of your new companion, you, as a responsible dog person, become accountable for it and its behavior. A dog that is taught to obey will automatically become a canine good citizen. As a canine member of your family, your Yorkie must learn to respect the feelings of others in its environment. You, as its guide, must help the dog establish good habits. Truly, if more owners would realize that their responsibility goes beyond just the basic daily care of their new family member, we would have fewer stray dogs roaming our neighborhoods, fewer dogs at our various rescue facilities, fewer dogs euthanized because of incompatibility, and less need for city and state legislation to control our pets.

Kindergarten Puppy Training (KPT)

Kindergarten Puppy Training (KPT) classes are a wonderful means of socializing your new family member. Puppies can be enrolled as early as eight weeks of age. When selecting a class, look for one where the instructor has had experience working with Toy breeds. Look for a small class that is not made up exclusively of larger breeds, so as not to overwhelm your little friend. Your puppy needs a lot of tender loving care at this time. It will retain more when its training sessions are short and pleasant. What will your pet learn in puppy kindergarten? Work will begin on getting and keeping its eye contact, which will help to establish a close relationship, or bonding, with you. Your puppy will be exposed to many different situations, and will have the opportunity to interact with other puppies and people. Joyce Anderson, of Raleigh, North Carolina, has trained both Yorkies and Lakeland Terriers in obedience. She begins with Kindergarten Puppy Training and feels that when training a small dog one must get down to its eye level to see things the way the dog sees them. She does admit, however, that this can make you look and feel a little crazy at times.

If you find that you and your Yorkie enjoy Kindergarten Puppy

Training, you may want to graduate to formal obedience classes. There is no reason why a four-pound Yorkie can't compete in the big leagues with German Shepherd Dogs and Golden Retrievers. As long as your Yorkie is a structurally sound, high-spirited worker with a good temperament and a willingness to please you, it can earn an obedience title.

Evaluating Classes and Trainers

Where does one start looking for a class or a trainer? Contacting a local obedience or all-breed dog club will probably produce some results. Many states have an organized Federation of Dog Clubs, which publishes an informational booklet listing breeders, clubs and classes. Check with your local veterinarian. Ask the breeder from which you purchased your dog about upcoming dog shows in your area. Plan to attend and talk with the obedience exhibitors about where they train. Once you know where classes are being held, arrange time to observe them. Most clubs welcome your interest in their programs.

Carli Bates, obedience instructor at the Cross Creek Dog Training Center in Glen Moore, Pennsylvania, suggests that you keep the following points in mind while observing a prospective class:

1. What training methods are used by the instructor? Training methods should not be excessively harsh. The correction should suit the dog's error, and it should always be followed by praise.
2. Is the instructor knowledgeable and organized? Is the class under control? A maximum of eight to ten handlers and dogs per instructor is ideal. If the class is larger, the instructor should have experienced assistants on hand to help out.
3. Are the training conditions suitable? The footing should not be slippery; if it is, rubber matting should be used. At the advanced level, the jumps should be in good condition. Above all, the atmosphere must be pleasant. The dogs should be working happily.

In some areas, a good training class can be hard to find. Many good obedience books have been written, which will help give you a better understanding of the various commands and and training techniques. However, they have their limits. Classes afford contact with other dogs, as well as one-on-one instruction, both of which are necessary to train a competitive working team.

The purpose of an obedience class is to train *you* to train your dog. Should Yorkie and you decide to venture off to school it will be most important to attend each and every session. There are beginners and advanced classes. At the first level, you will learn action exercises, such as heeling and coming on command, as well as control exercises, which involve sitting, standing, lying down and staying in one place. The exercises will begin on-leash, then progress to off-leash. Should you wish to continue at the advanced level, then exercises in retrieving, jumping, scent discrimination and hand signals will be introduced. Individual training and behavior problems also will be addressed during these sessions. To ensure a good working dog, it is not enough just to attend class. It will take short practice sessions at home as well. Always follow these sessions with some extra-special play time. Carole Klein, of Highland Lakes, New Jersey, who exhibits Yorkies in both breed and obedience, stresses the importance of ending your practice sessions on an up note. Always leave your dog feeling good about itself.

Obedience Competition—Right for You?

For those who decide to show in AKC Obedience Trials, there are three levels of competition: Novice, Open and Utility. The American Kennel Club publishes a booklet called *Obedience Regulations*, which may be obtained by writing to the American Kennel Club (see page 188). The importance of good sportsmanship both in and outside the ring is stressed in this booklet, which describes all obedience exercises and how they are to be performed as well as scored. Your dog must demonstrate willingness and enjoyment, and you must display a smoothness and naturalness—rather than military precision—while performing the exercises.

All dogs can be obedience trained. However, not all people have the personality, patience and ability to train their own dogs. If you find yourself in that category, but still wish to have an educated canine, you might consider locating a dog trainer who will train your dog either in your home, in class or both. Again, ask your dog's breeder or local kennel club for advice in finding such a person.

Over the years, there have been many good working obedience Yorkies. Lord Casey of Eastwood, UD (1978–90), will always be remembered by those who were fortunate enough to see him perform. What a magnificent working dog he was. Marjorie Davis, his owner and trainer, loves working her dogs in obedience. Each dog presents

Lord Casey of Eastwood, UD, owned and handled by Marjorie Davis, was a true star performer in obedience competition. Scoring High in Trial at the Yorkshire Terrier Club of America from 1982 through 1986, he is shown in the 1985 presentation under obedience authority and Yorkshire Terrier breeder-judge Merrill Cohen. *DiGiacomo*

Am., Can. Ch. Majestic Sir Henry Higgins, Am., Can. CDX owned and handled by Carole Klein, is shown here being awarded his American CDX degree by judge Patricia Scully at the Saw Mill River KC. According to Ms. Klein, Higgins is the only dog in the history of the breed to earn an obedience title and a breed championship on the same weekend. *John Ashbey*

her with a new challenge. She and Casey proved to be a great team. At age sixteen months, Casey began his career in the Novice class by taking a Second High in Trial, competing against more than 300 dogs, all breeds, with a score of 198. (In Obedience, each participant starts with a perfect score of 200 and points are deducted, depending on handler or dog errors.) In the Open class, his average score for eight years was 196 and in the Utility class it was 195. He had achieved sixty-five OTCH (Obedience Trial Championship) points when he had to be retired from jumping. Casey was top-winning obedience dog in the records of the Yorkshire Terrier Club of America from 1982–85, went High in Trial at the YTCA specialties from 1982–86, and ranked No. 1 Yorkie in obedience (Shuman system), 1982–84. He ranked sixth in the Top 10 Obedience Toys for 1983 (Shuman system). At age nine, Casey traveled with Marjorie to France to demonstrate obedience, Novice through Utility, to the Yorkshire Terrier Club of South France. At age eleven, Casey won the Veteran's class at the YTCA specialty with a score of 197½. Lord Casey proved that a five-pound dog can work just as well as one of larger size. He was welcomed at many nursing homes and was Marjorie's constant companion.

Davis' advice when training a Toy dog is to "remember that they are Toy dogs." They watch your feet a lot. Fast, small steps work best for her, along with constant talking and praise while training. She warns that the terrier nature makes Yorkshires a bit more challenging to train in obedience, because of their independent natures. Just when you think they have an exercise down pat, they decide to put on their own show, which is why a sense of humor is so important in working with this breed.

Controversy over whether one should show in conformation and obedience at the same time goes on and on. Most obedience instructors and exhibitors feel that it does not create a problem. Should you wish to do both, always let your obedience and conformation instructors know that you are training for both. Then the necessary steps can be taken from the beginning to avoid problems. Different collars and leashes, as well as different commands, will be used.

Carole Klein's Am. & Can. Ch. Majestic Sir Henry Higgins, Am. & Can. CDX certainly offers proof that a dual title is possible. Higgins is the only Yorkie in the history of the breed to obtain an obedience title and a breed championship on the same weekend. He was ranked No. 1 Novice obedience Yorkie, as well as No. 23 in the conformation breed rankings, in the *1991 Yorkshire Terrier Annual*.

PRIDE AND PATRIOTISM VERY MUCH APPARENT—The drill team of Carole Klein and Am., Can. Ch. Majestic Sir Henry Higgins, Am., Can CDX (*left*) and Cynthia Blemaster and Se Mor's Little Charmer CD electrified the gallery at the Yorkshire Terrier Club of America's 1992 Specialty and later that same year they did it again at the Progressive Dog Club's all-Toy show. They put on a delightful performance combining precision obedience routines and marching skills set to the music of John Phillip Sousa's "Stars and Stripes Forever."

Higgins has had multiple Best of Breed and Group placings and multiple first-place Obedience wins. He is now working toward his Utility title. Another magnificent worker, also owned by Carole Klein is Can. OTCH Heskethane Sixpenny Bit, Am. UD. This Yorkie has a total of four Highest Scoring Dog in Trial awards and was the highest placing Toy in 1991 at the Gaines Eastern Regional competition in the Super Dog division. The key to Carole's training is a lot of verbal encouragement, keeping your dog motivated and tuned in to you. ''Be natural and use good foot work and make it look like fun'' for both you and your dog, she says.

Obedience can be whatever you wish. You may just want a well-behaved canine companion in the home, in public places and in the presence of other dogs. Or you may wish to spend time with your dog, meet new friends with a common interest and go to a few Obedience Trails close to home. You may become serious about it and decide to compete for the perfect score, traveling to trials around the country and earning an obedience title championship. Whatever you choose, foremost in your mind should be the quality, rather than the quantity, of time spent training your Yorkie. Here patience is very much a virtue.

There is nothing more wonderful than watching a Yorkie and its owner perform as a team. When Carole Klein, with her dog, Higgins, and Cynthia Blemaster and her Yorkie, Se-Mor's Little Charmer, CD, presented a salute to the Yorkshire Terrier Club of America at the 1992 Specialty, many spectators were moved to tears. This precision heeling and obedience routine, performed to the music of ''The Stars and Stripes Forever,'' concluded with the two Yorkies coming to heel at their owners' sides, miniature flags held gingerly between their teeth. An inspiring picture, indeed, of what obedience training can accomplish.

11

Caring for Your Yorkie

ALTHOUGH there are many books on dogs, both general and breed-specific, there is one book that we feel belongs on any Yorkie owner's bookshelf. This book, *All About Toy Dogs* by Viva Leone Rickets, published by Howell Book House, has what is lacking in many others. All directions, suggested first-aid care, and simple medications are figured to the correct size and dosage for Toy dogs. Unfortunately, the book is out of print and finding a copy will entail some digging.

The following on the psychology of the Toy dog is from *All About Toy Dogs* and so well describes our pal, the Yorkie, that we have included it here:

> The Toy dog is, for all intents and purposes, a big dog in a small package, the "compact car" of the canine world. Living as he usually does in the midst of his owner's household, he becomes one of the family in behavior and in his devotion to human beings. He scorns other dogs as companions, preferring his "family," and it is doubtful if he even knows that he is a dog!
>
> He jealously guards his domain, and he will fiercely attack any dog that comes along, whatever its size. He is not a "sissy" or a "pantywaist" as so many large-breed owners believe. The Toy dog walks tall, rough, tough and fierce in his own manner. He should be kept on a

leash when outside his home, and he is likely to challenge any dog he meets, flaunting his watchfulness and guardianship over his owners.

He is possessive of his bed, his toys and of anything he considers his property. He gets along well with other family pets, as long as they do not usurp first place in the affections of his owners, for he is quick to sense the emotions and affections of his loved ones.

A Toy dog soon learns to read his owner's intentions from his actions. He is rarely fooled, no matter how elaborate the attempts of his owner to deceive him. Such an attempt will only cause him to view other attempts with suspicion. Let him find a pill or other medicine in a ball of food just once, and thereafter he will take apart every ball of food handed him until his suspicions are lulled.

It is not that the Toy dog is smarter than the large breeds, but his close association with his human family provides him with a ''College Course'' in human behavior.

Toy dogs are very sensitive to tones of the human voice, and their responses are to this aspect of speech rather than to words. It is impossible, however, for any to live closely with a Toy dog over a length of time and not become convinced that they do know and understand the meaning of many words.

His actions, whether conscious or unconscious, his behavior in relation to his sensations, his emotions and his physical conduct will, in large measure, reflect the behavior pattern of his human family. If he lives in the midst of a noisy and excitable family, he is likely to be a noisy little dog conditioned to shrill and prolonged arguments. If his owners are on the quiet and dignified side, he will exhibit the same measure of serenity.

His feelings of closeness to his owners and of being a part of the family are the reasons he does not adapt well to being left at a boarding kennel when the family goes on vacation, or at a veterinarian hospital when ill. He feels deserted, but he grieves with a quiet dignity that human beings might well emulate. If left at a hospital for treatment of a serious illness, his inner sickness of heart may well defeat a veterinarian's best efforts.

It has been pointed out to us that not everybody thinks as we do. This does not exactly come as news. However, this section will have to be based to a great extent on our personal experiences. Indeed we were once beginners and, in our enthusiasm, have managed to fall into every bear-trap, near or far removed. Like all hobbies, these pitfalls, though grim at the time, really are experience teachers. The problems that confront the novice enthusiast are many, but as you progress you find the mountains diminish in height. Your Yorkie can be what you make of it, but first you need to know what, where, when and why.

On Buying a Yorkshire

What part is your Yorkie going to play in your scheme of life? Is it to be a show dog, obedience dog, or your companion? There is no earthly reason why a Yorkie can't fill all three jobs at once, just so long as your choice has the looks, intelligence and disposition to so perform.

If you plan to breed your Yorkie, then its size must be a consideration. Whether yours will be a limited breeding program, or a larger program, can be the determinant of which sex to choose for your first puppy.

A female comes in season usually twice a year. She should never be bred on her first season, or before a year, and preferably not until after eighteen months. She needs to grow up, to mature physically, mentally and emotionally. A young bitch may make a good mother, but the odds are against this. She is more likely to have weak puppies and, minus maturity, treat them as an encumbrance rather than with maternal devotion.

If you plan to show your bitch, it is best to gain her title before breeding her. Puppies do not assist in the cultivation of their dam's coat. Instead, they treat her long tresses more as a nesting bed or play tug-of-war with it. In the case of an extremely long coat, a Yorkie puppy can become entangled and strangle; or the mother may frantically chew at anything to untangle her pup, in the course of which she may seriously injure the puppy.

A bitch that is in season may not be shown in obedience, so if obedience is your main aim a male is probably what you should consider.

The size that you desire in your Yorkie should be considered before purchasing. A large male makes a wonderful family pet, able to bear up to and enjoy playing with children past the toddler age. He is a great companion for a single person, young or old, as is the very tiny Yorkie, either male or female. However, very small Yorkies are not good pets for small children.

For breeding purposes, size is of great importance. Nothing over seven pounds is desirable. A small male, if from small heritage, is a good choice. A tiny bitch (anything weighing under three and a half pounds) should never be bred. You, as a breeder, are the controlling force in your Yorkie's life. Therefore, you have a responsibility to not purposely endanger that life. A tiny bitch is not capable of naturally delivering a puppy. She will, in all probability, need a cesarean section, and with her tiny size the shock and stress may very well kill her.

The best size for breeding, showing or both is around five pounds. An oversized female will make a good brood, but her size must always be remembered in future generations, for, sure as shooting, that large bitch will turn up as an oversized male in the next generation. And let us hastily add that the very tiny stud dog will come out in future generations as a ''teacup'' bitch. This usually works out into one litter containing the last named bitch and the oversized male.

When your decision has been made on what you want, either show, breeding or pet, then you should really investigate and be careful of freely given advice of an adverse nature.

It is best, in our opinion, to buy your puppy from a breeder. If purchased from a breeder, you have the opportunity of seeing the puppy's dam and the sire, unless the dam was bred to a stud dog owned by someone else. You will also see other dogs, both youngsters and adults, that the breeder has bred.

In buying from a breeder, you can be sure of the environment in which your puppy was raised. You will have someone to help you with any problems that may come up. The breeder has the puppy's best interest at heart. If you do not know of a breeder in your area, you can write to the Secretary of the Yorkshire Terrier Club of America, Inc. for information on breeders, or write to the American Kennel Club, 51 Madison Ave., New York City, NY 10010. (The AKC can provide you with the name and address of the current secretary of the YTCA.) If there is a dog club in your town, you might get help through it. It is also possible that a veterinarian in your area can tell you where to look for a Yorkie.

Just like every other thing you buy, buying a name brand assures you of the product's reputation. A breeder has spent countless hours planning for the litter, days and nights taking care of the mother and young puppies. The breeder is attached to those puppies and you can be sure that selling one is almost like putting it out for adoption. Good breeders are usually extremely careful of where and to whom their puppies go.

It is best not to purchase a puppy under three months of age and,

Well-bred, well-reared puppies are a source of pride to their breeders and a source of joy to all whose lives they touch. These three-month-old babies by Ch. Shadomountin Upper Cut ex Ch. Steppin' Up Misbehavin' are shown here with Janet Jackson. *Don Petrulis*

if for show, preferably not under five or six months. The time of year in which you should purchase your Yorkie, is dependent on whether it is to be housebroken or trained to use newspapers indoors. If your climate is moderate all year around—don't worry about this. But deep snow, monsoon rains, or 100-degree temperatures outdoors are obviously not conditions under which to housebreak a Yorkie puppy. If these climatic deterrents prevail in your area, then wait to purchase the puppy until better weather is likeliest.

Having decided where to purchase, contact the breeder and make an appointment to see the dogs. Be sure you tell the breeder what you want. If it is a pet, explain what your family is like and what you expect of the dog in the way of personality. If you want a show dog, say so. No one, in Yorkies, ever got a great show dog by buying a pet. Breeders sell dogs as pets for a variety of reasons, but, if sold as a pet, the dog is not believed show-worthy. If you want to buy a show dog, we repeat, tell the breeder your true intent, and wait until one is available. Do not, in your enthusiasm and impatience, rush out and buy the first puppy you can obtain.

Follow these few do's and don'ts:

1. Always demand proof of AKC registration, and ask for a three-generation pedigree. If the AKC registration is in process, or not available, ask for the registration number of the sire and dam.
2. Make it a straight purchase—no strings attached, such as pick of first litter, etc.
3. If you can only obtain the animal by making some sort of breeding arrangement, put all the terms down in writing. One copy for each party involved, and be sure the agreement is legal and binding.
4. No matter how fine the breeding, don't buy a sickly puppy, or an extremely shy puppy. Either condition may be curable, but the scars may also last the Yorkie's entire lifetime.

The New Arrival

Having picked your puppy, be sure to get its medical record, including the name of the veterinarian who has been treating the breeder's dogs. This will help your own veterinarian if any questions should arise.

190

These ten-week-olds' ears have yet to come up.

At three months, these puppies by Ch. Doodletown Tom Tom ex Ch. Wildweir's Wicked Countess are growing and only one ear is still down!

Ask the breeder to give you full instructions on what the puppy has been eating, including how much, what type of dish and at what hours. A puppy used to a metal dish may refuse food from a china one and vice versa.

Upon arriving home, keep the puppy to one room. The whole new environment will be too much for the puppy to adjust to immediately. Don't give it food or water for at least an hour after it gets home. Let the newcomer meet the family, but hold off the neighbors and children's friends until the puppy has had a day to get used to its new home. The puppy is going to be tired from the excitement and change, so expect it to explore and then sleep.

Having chosen where the puppy will sleep, when bedtime comes put the puppy to bed. This should be a box, or metal bed to start with. A wood or wicker one is going to be demolished when the puppy cuts its permanent teeth. You might even consider a small wire crate for its bed. Most Yorkies like a place of their own to sleep in, to hoard their treasures in, or just to be able to watch the goings-on from. Whatever you choose for the bed, provide a towel, bathmat, rag rug, or old blanket in which your puppy can snuggle. Don't use anything made of polyester—the mat can get into the lungs, and it is toxic. Leave a bowl of clean water always available.

Sometimes a puppy, feeling lost and lonely, will whine and cry when left alone. Leaving a radio on low will give it a sound that is familiar in an environment that no longer contains its familiar sounds and smells.

We must admit that most Yorkies, be they pet or show dog, fail to see any reason why they should not share your bed—but that's an individual decision to be made by each owner. Or should that be each dog?

Care of the Female Yorkie

Like all dogs, Yorkie bitches vary as to when they will first come in season. The average age is between nine months and one year. Like all averages, there are exceptions and Yorkies have a great fondness for reading the footnotes at the bottom of pages concerning these exceptions. Hence they may come in season as early as seven months, or may wait till they are even twenty months old. We have found that some bitches will have a season prior to one year that is so immature that neither the owner, nor a male dog will be aware of the condition.

This fugitive season will usually be noticed only by a change in the bitch's personality, and an increased amount of licking around the vulva.

Most Yorkies will come in season twice a year, but occasionally one will come in season once a year, or even every eighteen months. If your bitch deviates too much from the norm, you should discuss it with your veterinarian, as he will be the best judge of whether there is a problem. Certainly any bitch that comes in season more than twice a year should be checked.

The average season lasts three weeks and, again, there are exceptions. Often, the first season may continue longer.

We have found that almost all Yorkies will have a false pregnancy after their first season. It does not necessarily indicate that something is wrong, and these bitches generally make very good mothers.

A false pregnancy occasionally will make a bitch grouchy, disinclined to eat, or lethargic. Patience and a little tender love will help her through this period more than anything else.

Most bitches will be ready to accept a male between the ninth and fourteenth days. There is always the rare bitch who must be mated before the ninth day, or one who must be mated very late in her season.

Never force a mating! Mother Nature has a way of protecting her children and, over a period of years, we have found that Yorkie bitches who are extremely difficult to mate will have whelping difficulties, or may even run into problems during their pregnancy.

Since most females are very fastidious about cleaning themselves, an unwary owner may have the bitch in season several days before he knows it. It is best always to count back one or two days when determining the proper day for breeding.

If you have more than one bitch, be careful that they do not develop an antagonism to each other when one is in season. Some bitches, when in season, are so inclined and should be given a place of their own at this period. If you do have a group of Yorkies, you are indeed asking for a fight if you allow this kind of a bitch to stay free with your others. For safety's sake, close her away from them.

Do not allow two males to be with a bitch when she is in season but not ready to be bred. Along with the fact that your calculations may be wrong on when to mate her, the two males are very likely to fight over her. For some reason we've never understood, people find it strange that occasionally Yorkies will get into a fight when a group are run together. It is best to realize that no one would consider running

Remember, breeding dogs—for all its many joys and satisfactions—has a generous share of pitfalls as well. So before breeding, be sure it is something you fully understand and are prepared for—responsibility and all.

five or six Terriers of any kind together, nor would they have five or six large dogs running together. Although a Yorkie is a small Toy dog, it is still a dog. Only dogs that are known to get along should be together when there is no one home. A bitch in season, a sick or a weak dog should never be left with a large group.

Care of the Bitch Prior to Whelping

Once you have bred your bitch and she is out of season, there is no reason to change her usual life-style. Exercise is necessary for her well-being. She should not be allowed to jump or climb stairs after the fourth week of her pregnancy. If she is used to traveling it won't hurt her so long as she has a crate to travel in, and you provide extra rest stops for her. Avoid travel if you can, but if you must, better to take her than to board her. Don't let her chase balls, or enter into strenuous activity.

She should be fed a diet rich in protein, and add milk or cottage cheese or calcium. Include a vitamin formula that you have discussed with your veterinarian. Most commercial vitamin preparations are calculated for ten-to-twenty-pound dogs. Your bitch weighs less than this, so ask your veterinarian about how much. Too large a dosage with vitamins is as bad as not enough (either way you are heading toward producing freaks). Remember that anything you feed or give your bitch goes into her bloodstream, and so feeds the fetus. Don't, for Heaven's sake, work on that old theory that what you don't provide the bitch, the puppies will get from her system. T'ain't so. Mother takes first! Don't allow her to be carried by others when she's pregnant, and as she advances in her pregnancy be sure she has a quiet, private place to rest.

Much has been written about making a whelping box, and having read some of the plans and descriptions for these accouterments, we're sure that our mothers have obviously not had luxury accommodations for their whelpings. Now if you are so inclined, and have the time and desire, go ahead with your carpentry. You can even add lace, ribbons, rattles and pink or blue blankets and your future mother-to-be will probably love it. However, we have found that a trip to the grocery store for several paper cartons is easier and far more sanitary in the long run.

You will need at least two—one for the bitch to whelp in, and another to move her and babies into after the whelping is over. The boxes that canned goods or beer come in are ideal. Never use one that has contained detergents, abrasives or poisonous material. Cut an opening on one side, so that the box makes a basket-type bed. Leave a strip on the side about two and a half to three inches high to keep the puppies from tumbling out.

Having decided where you'd like the whelping to take place, let your future mother have the box to sleep in ahead of time. With luck, she'll agree it's a great place, rather than your bed, or under the couch. Small, easily washed terry-cloth dish towels or flannel baby receiving blankets make excellent bedding for the box.

You will need for the whelping: disinfectant, clean towels to dry the puppies with, paper towels, scissors, and dental floss, which you'll find excellent for tying any cords that need to be tied. Be sure to let your veterinarian know that the whelping date is coming up.

There is no more important person in deciding to become a breeder than your veterinarian. Without him, or her, you are lost. No kennel has ever gotten to the top without a veterinarian's help. We know of no breeder who would not agree with us that without trust and respect for your veterinarian you cannot continue. It is their good judgment and patience that help us through the various trials that ensure in the course of raising dogs.

It is best to make your plans and your mind up for the night party which will probably occur when your bitch whelps. For some mysterious reason, best known to themselves, this is the most popular time for having puppies.

There are dozens of very good books, by medical authorities, on how to whelp your bitch, so we will confine ourselves here to a few comments pertaining to the Yorkshire Terrier.

Some bitches will carry the puppies beyond the expected date for whelping. If this does occur, the bitch should be taken to the veterinarian to be examined to be sure all is O.K. We have found that it is best not to wait more than twenty-four hours after the due date from the last day of mating. If she does not whelp by this time, in our opinion and from some experience, a cesarean should be performed. Waiting longer may prove fatal for the puppies.

Once your Yorkie has started into actual labor, that is, actually bearing down and trying to deliver a puppy, you may allow two hours for the first to arrive. If this time elapses without a puppy appearing, your veterinarian should be contacted.

Care of the Puppies and New Mother

When you have a happy mother with her litter, see that all the puppies are nursing, but, unless there is a weak puppy, keep your hands off! Leave her alone. Since Yorkies have relatively small litters, you will have enough nipples (or teats) to go around. All that fussing and cussing you hear is just one of the pups squashing everyone aside to get to its choice nipple. Puppies will pick out a favorite nipple right from birth, always heading for that special one when hungry. If you interfere by trying to have the puppies nurse on a nipple of your choice, they usually get upset, refusing to suck. If the litter is large and there is a weak puppy, then you are going to have to help and do a little pushing for this weaker puppy. But let the others get their favorite places and then give the weak puppy the leftover spot.

A loving pat and a bit of praise on her performance are all that ''Mom'' requires from you at this time. She should have a bowl of water and, if she has not eaten, give her a bowl of her usual food. All the books we have ever read assure us that a bitch won't eat twelve hours prior to whelping. We have found that our own bitches really cannot see any reason to pass up a meal, so they eat all meals and proceed to whelp after, between and around mealtimes.

If you are coping with a bitch that has had a cesarean, here are a few hints that will help. We must state right here, that as we have, in our opinion, the best veterinarians in the United States, we do not have some of the problems other breeders have reported to us. Almost all of our bitches are awake from the anesthetic and caring for their puppies within two hours of the actual operation.

In a litter born by cesarean section, remember that these pups will be slower starting. Settle the mother at one end of the box, on her side, and put the puppies in the center of the box so they can reach the nipples. Place a hot water bottle, or heating pad on ''low'' at the other end of the box. This way the puppies can nurse and lie on the warmth of the bottle, or pad, thus relieving the pressure from where Mom is sore. Do everything you can to get the mother to assume her chores. She hurts and will, if given the chance, let you take on all her chores. Don't do it! Close your ears, partially harden your heart. If the pups are not nursing, gently open their mouths and gently get a nipple well into the puppy's mouth, squeezing a drop into its mouth. Leave their front feet free to pump the breast. The milk the puppies get at first will have some of whatever anesthetic was used so the puppies will be more sluggish than a natural-born litter. This first milk has the colostrum that is necessary for natural immunity.

A bitch who has had a cesarean should be kept beside you for at least twelve hours and longer if she is not fully recovered and wide awake. You may have to rescue the puppies from time to time if they get behind their mother, as she may be too sleepy to move. Your bitch should be turned over every hour until she takes over moving about on her own. Ice cubes should be offered for her thirst, and, if you do give her water, be sure it is in very small amounts until she is wide awake. If she does not show signs of returning to full consciousness after twelve hours, she should be taken to see your veterinarian.

Should she be the rare Yorkie mother, or an extremely spoiled pet who wants no part of the whole thing, try placing the box with the puppies, mother and hot water bottle or heating pad inside a wire crate. Cover the top sides, but not the ends, with towels to block any drafts. This covered crate seems to give reassurance and serves to prevent that one bitch, because she is scared and sore, from leaving the babies.

As we have said, all mothers like a bit of praise on their performance, but if the bitch is your only one, be sure that you give her extra love and praise before touching her puppies. She can get jealous of her babies if she is used to being the center of attention.

The question of the temperature in the room where the litter is kept always comes up. We have found that our newborn puppies and their mothers do best if the area they are in remains at around 78 degrees, winter and summer. This means that in summer the room is air conditioned. The mother and puppies should be situated so that they are not in a draft. Since not everyone agrees on what is the proper temperature, we can only suggest you discuss it with your own veterinarian.

If you have weathered the first three or four days and still have a puppy that is not thriving—one that has a high-pitched constant whining cry and is cold to the touch—you can try everything you want, but, in all probability, we hate to tell you, this one won't make it. If you wish to try your luck at hand-raising, consult your veterinarian for suggestions and instructions. However, all your fussing over the high-pitched whining puppy will upset the dam and the other puppies, so be careful. When it does go, don't blame yourself; Yorkies are little animals and sometimes Mother Nature doesn't get things put together in the right order in these puppies.

A few bitches will not eat, or eat lightly, twelve to twenty-four hours, occasionally forty-eight hours, after whelping. As long as they have no abnormal temperature, and act normal otherwise, there is nothing to worry about. Once your bitch starts eating, and we must say most do once the family is settled and nursing, her appetite and her needs for calcium, phosphorus and vitamin D climb rapidly. You will need to give her a good ratio of a dietary balance of calcium-phosphorus to avoid eclampsia.

Eclampsia is caused by a temporary imbalance of the calcium metabolism and usually shows up two to three weeks after whelping. It can come earlier, or even in the prenatal period. For three weeks after whelping a bitch needs two to three times as much nourishment as at any other period. She should receive a meal of fresh milk, evaporated milk or cottage cheese.

After nursing, most bitches are low or even lacking in calcium, and may also have depleted other necessary vitamins and minerals while producing milk. Therefore, they should be fed back into condition as soon as possible.

What type of calcium-phosphorus, vitamin D and extra vitamins and minerals are to be used, should be discussed with your veterinarian.

Tails and Dewclaws

Tails should be docked and dewclaws removed by your veterinarian between the third and sixth days after birth. (For the uninitiated, dewclaws are the extra functionless toes on the inside of the leg.)

It is always advisable to remove dewclaws, back and front, though their presence is not a fault. Their presence can be a problem when grooming. If they are not removed, be sure to keep the nails trimmed short.

Weaning

When the puppies are about three weeks old, slide your hand (palm side up) around and under the puppies and you will find that they start licking your fingers. Now they are ready for food. Because they will not be able to stand on their feet, you need a dish that will

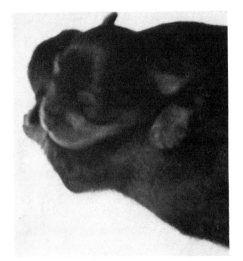

One day old. Note tan points on heads and paws.

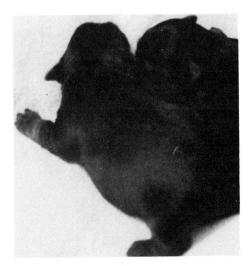

One day old—side view.

One day old—viewed from the end of the as-yet-undocked tail.

At a week-and-a-half, Jeanne Grimsby's puppies' eyes are still tightly shut.

At three-and-a-half weeks life can be so demanding.

fit under the lower jaw, but still leave room for their front feet to push at. They won't realize it at first, but this new food doesn't need pumping. With our Yorkies we have found that the glass casters that are made to put under the legs of tables or couches to protect the rugs, are absolutely perfect first dishes for the puppies. They don't slide, and the edge gives the puppies a chance to suck, slurp and finally chew the food out. To give the puppy an idea, gently push its chin and front feet into the food in the glass caster, or place a little food in its mouth so that it can get a taste of the food. If the puppy isn't interested in this treat, wait a couple of days. Don't force it. Puppies differ in their desire for food. One pup may feel that mother's milk is sufficient long after the rest of the crew consider it only sauce for their other food.

What should you start your puppies on? Well, we can only suggest what we've found successful, and that is raw hamburger, the one that the grocery sells as neither round nor chuck. Next, give them small-curd cottage cheese in a separate glass caster. Cottage cheese is higher in protein than milk, and the latter is a glorious source of diarrhea in dogs of all ages.

It is unfortunately true that the raising of puppies is not all clear sailing. It is, by far, better to anticipate the condition before your puppies are too weak to be saved. Remember, that all points in the rearing of puppies that involve any change will create stress. Any indication of an infection, whether bacterial or viral, indicates a speedy trip to the veterinarian.

The times most important to watch for symptoms of stress are in the first week of weaning, especially if the dam has been totally removed from her puppies. This usually occurs when the mother's milk has soured or the dam calls it quits. Any puppy that is lying too quietly, or has loose bowel movements calls for quick action. We have found, with suggestions from our veterinarians, that a gentle deterrent, like children's Kaopectate, should be administered, with a digestible (charcoal tablets—an eighth is about right for the average three-to four-week old puppy) helping to keep down the formation of gas. One a day is the usual, but sometimes you may need a second dose. A dropper of honey, mixed with cooled, boiled water and a tiny bit of calcium twice a day, helps to bring things back right. A drop or two of a baby formula vitamin won't hurt and will probably help.

In the case of colic, vomiting or a stomach distended with gas, use an infant suppository cut down to size that will fit a puppy's rectal opening. Gently administer it; don't shove it way in. This will stimulate

202

the puppy to relieve itself and pass some of the gas. Pepto-Bismol (children's), administered with a dropper in dosage of about a quarter teaspoon two or three times, and a digestible, usually brings this right. The charcoal acts in the stomach as a sponge to absorb the gas.

If the puppy's stomach is hard and distended, it is best to seek medical advice. If possible, you should have in your dog's medical cabinet medicine that will reduce the pain associated with colic. It must be approved by your veterinarian and figured for a puppy weighing as little as one pound.

While your Yorkie is cutting either its puppy (milk) teeth or adult permanent teeth, something hard to chew on is advisable. This is where the great American baby food industry is helpful. Look in the baby food section and bring home some of those "teething biscuits" or whatever the latest call name for them may be. If the puppies are turning their noses up at cottage cheese, it is wise to add your veterinarian's recommended dosage of a calcium product. *DO NOT* select your own. Too much calcium, minus the corrective vitamins, can cause more woe than you will ever wish for. As teeth cutting is a stress on the entire system of your puppy, a little extra dextrose in the form of honey, Karo syrup or even malted milk tablets won't hurt and it may help avoid the stress syndrome.

Baby vitamins, in small dosage, are helpful to the weak puppy. You should discuss with your veterinarian as to what is the right vitamin and mineral product to add to all your Yorkie's diet. Also, how much per pound of body weight and the amount to increase for pregnant bitches and weaned puppies.

A little Vaseline (petroleum jelly) smeared on the puppies' tailends will help to prevent a bowel movement from becoming stuck to the hair. Although the puppies will be able to cope with proper bowel elimination once they no longer have mother's tongue, occasionally one will get caught due to one of a number of circumstances. Excess hair, trimmed from around the rectum, will also help to prevent this problem.

How often should you feed the puppies? In the early stages we remove the mother from the puppies, let the puppies that wish to eat get their fill, and then let the mother back in to clean up what's left. Sometimes this doesn't work and Mom gets too much food.

It should be pointed out that a single puppy is usually slower to be weaned than are puppies from a larger litter. By the time the pups are five or six weeks old, the food should be given to them and left with them. Change it after three hours or so to keep it fresh. It should not be offered at some dictated hour only. Their small systems, like those of birds, use more food for energy than their size shows. Also, each puppy differs in its ability to assimilate the food it takes in.

About this age, try offering the puppies some hamburger simmered in a small amount of water. As the days progress, add a small amount of the same food you intend to feed the puppies as adults. Do not try to feed the puppies in separate dishes. You can do this, but all they do is switch dishes, so why knock yourself out? The idea is to provide food at all times so that each puppy can get nourishment when its small body needs it.

We have always allowed the mothers to play with their pups and to let them nurse as long as Mom says it is O.K. This seems to satisfy both mothers and puppies, and allows them to gain a sense of security, as well as instruction in all matters concerning doggy habits.

Provide a bowl of fresh water for the puppies at all times. Be sure the bowl isn't so deep that the puppies could fall in and drown and it must be low enough for them to drink from.

Shots

Until your puppy has had its vaccinations, don't take it where strange dogs have been, or allow it to be played with by anyone who has influenza or common cold symptoms. Children, having infectious diseases such as measles, mumps, etc., should never be close to a puppy. After a year there may be no harm, but it is best to consult your veterinarian. There are those who feel that dogs are immune to these diseases. In our opinion and with a bit of experience, we have found that since Yorkies are agreeable to being cuddled and willing to sympathize with the invalid, that the close association may very well bring the puppy down with a virus-type sore throat. Yorkies can show an inability to tolerate permanent vaccination prior to three months of age. Therefore extreme caution should be taken if necessary to vaccinate before this age.

Canine hepatitis is not the same as human hepatitis and neither can be transmitted from dog to human or vice versa.

If you do have to board your dog at a boarding kennel, it should have a booster shot in advance, so consult your vet. Don't board any puppy under six months, and, if avoidable, don't board a puppy at all. This booster shot, prior to boarding, may very well save you a case of "kennel cough" or in fancier terms, tracheobronchitis. This is a cough that sometimes brings up a little mucus with it. The cough usually doesn't bother the dog as much as it worries the owner. However, if left untreated, it can get worse and can develop into a more serious ailment. Prompt treatment by your veterinarian will usually see this cough cured in about two weeks or less.

A booster may also be wise if you are traveling with your Yorkie and this should be discussed with your veterinarian.

If properly administered and from a reputable drug firm, there should be no danger having your Yorkie vaccinated for rabies. Most states require this by law, and for your dog's protection, it is advisable. *DO NOT* use the three-year vaccine which must be injected intramuscularly and is, therefore, somewhat more painful than the one-year vaccine which is given under the skin (subcutaneously). There have been cases in large dogs of lameness afterward, and the injection site on a Yorkie is far, far too small for this type of vaccine.

Feeding After Three Months

When your puppy is around three months old, start it on food in a separate dish and get it onto three regular feeding times. As soon as it cuts its second (permanent) teeth, usually around four and a half months, the puppy should be put on two meals a day. Yorkies should remain on two meals all of their lives. Due to their small size, one meal is inadequate. With two, a Yorkie can better utilize its food.

What to feed your Yorkie? The manufacturers of dog foods spend millions of dollars on their products, producing tested and researched food for dogs. It is highly unlikely that anyone can make up a better balanced meal for a dog in their kitchen. The breeder from whom you purchase your dog will gladly explain what, when and how much your puppy is used to being fed, and suggest substitutions should the product they use not be available in your area. If you want to add table scraps to the dog food product, go ahead, it won't hurt. But you'll have a happier, healthier Yorkie if you give it dog food.

Most Yorkies are very good eaters and if they are not, there is usually a physical or emotional reason involved. On average, a Yorkie needs one level tablespoon of food for each pound of body weight at each meal—hence a four-pound Yorkie needs about four level tablespoonfuls per meal. Obviously some require more or less, depending on activity or temperament.

While your puppy is teething, it may want its food mashed up

At three months, this puppy shows good balance and a proper head for his age. *Ritter*

This six-month-old puppy will develop a desirable silky coat. Puppies that grow up to have good coats will often show a sparse coat at this awkward age.

fine, or even handed to it piece by piece, especially while its front gums are swollen. If it doesn't eat a meal, don't panic—it may have a slight upset. However, if it is actually in distress, or persistently refuses food, a visit to the veterinarian is called for. Yorkies can develop extremely serious colic due to the stress caused by the pain, so it should be attended to if necessary. Tempting your Yorkie with roast beef and chicken is fine if your veterinarian says to do so, but making a habit of these goodies will be producing a bad eater.

Teething

Yorkies usually start cutting their second or permanent teeth at around three months. The baby teeth will start to loosen as the permanent teeth, coming through from below, push their way up. The mouth should be checked two or three times a week once the teeth start coming in, as a baby tooth can become wedged tight by two permanent teeth coming through at the same time. This can cause crooked teeth, or throw the whole bite out of line. A baby tooth often becomes capped on top of the permanent tooth, and it should be removed either with your fingers, a pair of tweezers or dental forceps.

One of the greatest teething problems in the breed is failure to lose the first set of canines. Often a puppy will retain both sets of canines. The cause is one which traces to the breed's origin. Being rat terriers, the canines have very long roots and as the second canine comes in, it will often work as a brace preventing regular play and chewing actions from loosening the first canine. Should this happen, it may be necessary to have a veterinarian remove the puppy set, especially if they are interfering, or in any way, causing the teeth to come in so as to ruin the dog's correct bite. If they are not, we do not advise taking the risk involved with surgical removal. In time they generally loosen and can be removed by the owner, or will fall out themselves. Keep a close watch on these canines as they come in, as there is quite often a point when they are loose and can be removed before they become wedged tight.

The corner of a washrag, or a gauze pad, dampened and dipped in baking soda and then rubbed over the teeth once a week will help keep tartar from forming. Toothpaste makes too much foam for a dog's mouth, and should not be used.

Training and Socializing

Along with proper selection and breeding stock, proper mating, proper feeding and proper medical care, there is still one more "proper" left in order to arrive at a well-adjusted adult dog. That is, proper training and socializing.

A puppy that just grows, never getting more attention than being fed and cleaned, is simply never going to have the personality to be a well-adjusted companion or show dog. No matter how great a Yorkie's attributes are, if it is scared and shy, it does not represent the correct temperament for the breed.

A shy dog will never make a good show dog. A show dog is expected to be just that—"a dog that shows off its temperament, type and soundness." There are occasionally dogs that do not enjoy shows, that simply refuse to give their all, even though they have had every bit of proper training, or socializing.

Each puppy should have its own "call name" by six weeks and the name should be used when touching or playing with the puppies. Never give your dog a name that sounds like the word, or words, that you use to censure your dog. A dog named "Beau" cannot tell that you are not saying "No," nor can one named "Pop" tell when you're saying "Stop." It confuses the dog, and to be safe, it will fail to respond to your call.

Puppies should have small rubber toys to play with in their puppy pens. Small "Nylabones," or hard rubber bones, are good as they can chew on these when cutting a tooth.

Put the puppies out for short periods to explore and investigate the area around their pen. Be sure that nothing scares them, but don't overprotect them. Extend the time that they are out playing in the room, and let their mother play with them. She gives them a sense of security at first and, as time progresses, she'll start playing with them. Let her, even though it may look rough to you. The puppies will roughhouse, engage in mock battles, and chase each other. This type of play is normal development for terriers, and should only be interfered with if one puppy appears to consistently get the worst of these games. An old nylon stocking with several knots tied in it will keep everyone busy.

Take time to play with the puppies yourself. Even if your puppy is not to be a show dog, it is still entitled to the proper development of its mind and body. Sit down on the ground and let them explore this large, friendly giant that is their boss.

Yorkies love to play and can easily be taught to swim. The frolicking puppy shown below is just eight weeks old.

As they grow up, introduce them to other areas of the house, the grass, and other outdoor surfaces. A puppy that has not learned about different surfaces can balk when suddenly confronted with a strange surface it has never seen or felt.

One of the statements most often made by those who do not know Yorkies, or for that matter, Toy dogs, is that they are afraid they'll step on them. Well that's one thing all Yorkies learn at an early age, if they've had any attention. Once they are on the floor, experience teaches them to move out of the way of advancing human feet. You can avoid having to comfort the sufferer of a stepped-on paw by going barefoot a few times when you first put the puppies out to explore. After being bumped by your foot once or twice, they learn to get out of the way.

Because Yorkies are small, one is tempted to pick them up to pet them and there is no reason not to do so. However, the chance is that, at sometime, a judge or a visitor to your home will lean down to touch your dog. If your dog has not been accustomed to someone doing this, it will probably lie down flat or shy away. So lean over the puppies sometimes to pat them, run your hand down their backs and scratch their tailends. The puppies will enjoy it and will grow up expecting such an event. After all, when you're as small as a Yorkie and it has never happened before, and a large human giant suddenly leans over toward you, you can hardly be blamed for moving away.

Because Yorkies are close to their human families, most of them will respond better if treated at home when ill. Occasionally, for a very ill dog, this may entail a daily trip to your veterinarian. But sick Yorkies feel safer and happier at home, so, if possible to make such arrangements, we can only advise that you do.

The Elderly Dog

Because of the long length of life enjoyed by Yorkies (usually thirteen to fifteen years, and some have lived to twenty years) we have included this section.

There unfortunately comes to each of us a moment when we are forced to realize that our little one is getting old. No longer does it see as well, or hear as it did. It sleeps most of the time and it may take a touch to waken rather than the sounds that woke it easily before.

This is the time to give it that extra help—a soft bed in the center of things, where it can lie and watch its favorite world. It will feel drafts faster now, and with the stiffness in its joints will enjoy warmth. Because of the stiffness, your Yorkie will not be able to bend as well to keep itself clean. A damp rag or sponge should be used to clean up the area where it urinates. Keep its eyes cleaned with a clean damp rag, or tissue, as they will run more now. It may be necessary to wipe around its mouth after it has eaten.

Should your Yorkie develop bladder trouble, or should simple old age make necessary frequent eliminations, a thick pad of newspaper around its bed will help and make things easier for you. If your old dog makes a mistake, admonishing it will only make its troubles worse.

Short slow walks, or rambles in the yard, are good for it, but don't tire your old friend. If the weather is cold, your dog will need a sweater, or raincoat. If your Yorkie gets damp, dry it well.

Your Yorkie should have the proper kind of vitamins made for older dogs. It will need medical attention more often, if it is to enjoy life. Blind dogs can adjust to their problem and, often, a young dog will assist. We've seen some of our oldest dogs taken on as the responsibility of a two or three year old.

Answering the Most Often Asked Questions

This section is a medley of useful somethings that may help in a pinch, or possibly avert a tragedy. It includes answers to the questions on caring for your Yorkie that we have found are most often asked by new owners, or would be owners, as well as some advice.

The Yorkshire Terrier is a charming house pet but, like all animals, never feels like developing worrisome problems until the wee small hours of the new day; 2:45 A.M. to 3:45 A.M. can seem like a whole calendar year when your Yorkie has that woebegone ''Please help me'' look! If the problem is an obvious medical one requiring emergency care, don't hesitate to call your veterinarian.

But, sometimes, there is a question in your mind as to whether it is an emergency. If your dog is bleeding, unconscious, convulsing, in shock, paralyzed, or has an extremely high or low temperature, it's ... emergency. The normal temperature, when taken rectally, is 101 degrees. An excited dog can easily get to 102 degrees but, above that, your dog should see its doctor. Some Yorkies, for reasons best known

"Wonder if they know as much about me as I know about them."

Yorkie puppies DO get up close and personal.

The Yorkshire Terrier is a photographer's delight.

All Yorkies curl their tongues up when panting.

to them, run a temperature between 100 degrees to 101 degrees normally. However, if the temperature is subnormal, below 99 degrees, the Yorkie needs immediate attention. Low, subnormal temperatures usually indicate shock, or poisoning from some cause. To make things easier for yourself, take your dog's temperature when it is well and happy. Then you will know when it is above, below or normal. Always take it before calling your veterinarian—it will help guide the doctor in determining what is the problem.

If you are totally at a loss as to what is wrong, go ahead and call the breeder. A dedicated breeder will gladly help even if it is the crack of dawn. If it can wait till morning, fine—but otherwise, that invention of Alexander Graham Bell's will probably render immediate assistance. A breeder has probably run into the problem or, if not, he'll know someone who has that he'll be glad to call.

However, use the same common sense you'd use for yourself. Most simple Yorkie ailments will respond to the same medicines you can give, or use on, an infant.

The best way to take care of an accident is to avoid it. Therefore, before you bring your new Yorkie home, check your house for those things that can cause tragedy. Follow these few simple precautions.

Indoor Precautions

All detergents and caustic cleansers should be out of the reach of the mouths of curious Yorkies. Puppies will chew on anything and the corners of boxes fit very nicely into their mouths. Should your Yorkie chew on something of this sort, grab dog and container and call your veterinarian. Most boxes of this kind carry directions for the immediate actions to be taken.

All poisons or anything that can cause harm should, in fact, be placed in an area or at a height where they are unattainable to your Yorkie.

No problem is more urgent for any dog owner than the immediate care that needs to be given a Yorkie that has eaten a chemical poison. It may be only a matter of minutes before the systemic effects of this poisonous compound begin and permanent damage to the internal organs result.

Many chemicals which an animal may ingest can be harmful and even fatal. These products are found in rodenticides, plant insecticides, lead-based paints, gasoline, antifreeze, amphetamine compounds, arsenical agents found in many animal bathing solutions, kerosene products used for insecticides, mothballs, laundry and cleaning products.

Treatment of chemical poisoning needs quick action so call your veterinarian immediately. The time taken to get your Yorkie to the hospital allows time for further absorption of the poison.

Vomiting must be induced if the agent was eaten. This can be accomplished either by placing a teaspoonful of salt in the back of your dog's mouth, or giving it one or two teaspoonfuls of hydrogen-peroxide solution orally. Repeat the procedure in five minutes if no vomiting occurs.

If corrosive materials have been spilled on your dog's skin, flush the area with lots of water. If your Yorkie is hyper-excitable, or convulsing, protect it from injuring itself. Get your Yorkie to the veterinarian, your own if possible, otherwise any veterinarian, as fast as possible.

Do not allow your Yorkie to sleep near the stove if there is a chance of hot fat spattering on the dog. Don't carry boiling liquids across the kitchen if Yorkies are underfoot. If hot fat or liquid gets on the Yorkie, turn off the stove, put the pan or container down, catch your Yorkie and flood the area with cold water while dialing your veterinarian.

All garbage should be well out of the way. There is nothing like a ramble through the contents when your Yorkie is bored. But the ramble, in addition to making a terrible mess, may well be its last. Should your dog feast on garbage, get it to the veterinarian immediately.

Medicine of any kind should also be out of the Yorkie's reach. If you have any medication to take, it is wiser to place it in a drawer and shake the pills, tablets, capsules out of the container over and into the drawer. If one escapes your grasp, it will then fall into the drawer and not into the open receptacle below that is a Yorkshire Terrier's mouth. If, by chance, it does get one, dial your veterinarian, bottle in one hand and Yorkie in the other. If you can't get your veterinarian, call the pharmacy that filled the prescription and find out if you need to take action and, if so, what.

Never leave a Yorkie enclosed alone in a bathroom with a full tub of water. The Yorkie probably won't jump into it (unless you are in it!) but why chance it? Yorkies can swim very nicely and thoroughly

A fall or a leap, even from a low object, can result in serious injury for a Toy dog. Even if your Yorkshire can jump, be very cautious and never leave it unattended where an accident can result.

Check your entire house for anything potentially dangerous to your Yorkshire. Be particularly careful about house-plants. Many species can be toxic, especially to such a small dog.

215

enjoy doing so, but they can also panic like anyone who falls into deep water.

Any potted plant should be checked out to be sure that no part of it is poisonous. Even if placed high, leaves and blooms will fall. You may be a meticulous housekeeper, but your Yorkie is an automatic vacuum cleaner!

There are more than 700 types of plants that are poisonous or injurious to dogs. Since the list is far too long to include here, our best advice is don't let your Yorkie eat, or chew on plants, or bushes. In some plants only part is poisonous, such as the berries, the leaves, the root or the bulb. The poisonous content may also vary with the stage of development. The amount that must be ingested to produce serious symptoms or even death varies from plant to plant.

Nor should your Yorkie drink from any water that has algae on it; if in the woods, avoid all mushrooms and any of the fungus tribe.

A new puppy should be watched to be sure that it does not decide to practice chewing on any electric plug or cords. Our feeling on this is that any Yorkie caught at this activity deserves a loud ''No!'' and swift slap. Those little teeth through the cord are the instant commencement of death. If the dog goes into shock, it'll rarely ever be brought around and usually the voltage will be enough to kill.

One of the most useful items to a Yorkie owner is a bottle of that pungent condiment sauce made from a species of very hot red pepper. This sauce does not stain and washes off, but clings to whatever it is applied to. Your Yorkie will have a hot mouth for a few minutes after the first try. The second try will need only a sniff. It works well on electric cords, or on anything you do not wish it to try its teething on. Although the best bet is to teach it what not to chew on, young puppies when teething or cutting their second teeth are very persistent. This method will save you a lot of breath and possible damage.

Never leave your Yorkie up on furniture alone until you are sure it can get off it safely. Whoever is on the phone, or at the door, can wait while you avoid an accident (such as a broken bone or fractured skull) by taking the time to lift your Yorkie off before answering. For the same reason, do not leave a puppy alone near a flight of stairs unless you know it can negotiate them both ways—up and down.

Upstairs, downstairs and all around the house check for possible pitfalls or mishaps and you'll have no need to cry over an accident that could have been avoided.

Outdoor Precautions

Never allow your Yorkie outdoors when the lawn is being mowed. Your dog is too small for the person to see and they move extremely fast. A stone, or stick thrown out by a rotary mower could cause an injury, or fatality.

Walking should *always* be on a lead. Dogs hit by cars while accompanying their owners are, alas, always dogs that had never run into the road before.

Carrying a Yorkie in your arms should always be done with your fingers around a front leg, ready to tighten their hold in case your dog decides on a leap. A sore leg is better than a serious injury.

Don't leave your Yorkie alone in the car parked in a shopping center. Too many dogs have been stolen in this manner.

If you have a fenced yard, do not leave your Yorkies out in it alone, unless the whole yard is visible to you and you are watching. Many have been stolen in this manner, or have slipped out a tiny hole. Also, service people are unfortunately not known for their care in closing gates; for that matter, children forget too often, too.

If your dog should be lost or stolen:

1. Call the police and give them a description, etc.
2. Notify the Veterinarian Association in your area.
3. Notify all dog clubs in your area, as well as other breeders.
4. Notify your local cab, bus company, newspaper delivery service, and garbage collection service.
5. Ask your public utility meter readers to keep a lookout.
6. Place notices on bulletin boards in grocery stores and schools.
7. Ask the Boy Scouts, Girl Scouts, 4-H Clubs, etc., to watch out for your missing Yorkie.

Be sure they understand that they should notify you or the police, and that *unless* the dog comes to them they should not try to catch it. A lost dog, friendly as it may be, will panic and snap in its fear. If frightened, it may run into the path of a car.

Should your Yorkie break a leg while you are more than twelve hours away from a veterinarian, there is a simple way to protect it until you can get to a vet. Take the cardboard tube from the center of the toilet paper, or paper towels. Gently, but not too tightly, wrap the leg in cotton, or even toilet paper, leaving room for swelling. Slip the tube over the wrapped leg extending the tube so that the dog will walk on the end of it, thus putting no pressure on the leg. Try to keep it as quiet as possible until you can get to the veterinarian.

Toys

A Yorkie's toys should not be such as it is able to swallow, or that have small pieces that can be removed and swallowed. Soft rubber squeaky toys, hard rubber bones or balls, and Nylabones are all fine. Soft rubber balls will be demolished. All squeakers will probably be unsqueaked, but even unsqueaked they are fun.

A Final Caution

Yorkshire Terriers must be treated with extreme caution when administering any form of anesthetics. Therefore, if your dog is going to have one, be sure your veterinarian is well aware of this matter. Many Yorkies have died from overdoses of anesthetics. If your veterinarian is in doubt on this subject, ask him to consult a veterinarian who has worked with the breed. You may have to pay for a long distance call, but you'll have a live dog. If your veterinarian—and it'll be a mighty rare one—won't listen, go elsewhere.

As to the question of when should you put a dog to sleep, no one can give a positive answer. There comes a time when advancing helplessness, pain or necessity will dictate the answer. It is hard to realize, but true, that often our refusal to carry out this kindness to a suffering animal is actually a refusal on our part to face the grief that will be caused by losing our friend. Our ability to do this for our dogs is a duty given to us that we are unable to perform for some loved human that we must watch suffer in pain, and linger on when there is no possible hope.

Many people, feeling the hurt of parting from their Yorkie, shy off purchasing another. Many of these will succumb in a week or a month to a new Yorkie puppy. We have found that, because Yorkshire Terriers are such individuals, the best cure for this grief of losing your old friend is a new puppy.

Traveling with Your Yorkie

The one purchase we feel every Yorkie owner should make is a crate. Many new owners look askance until they've tried it. Their feeling is that they couldn't be so mean as to close up their dog in such a thing. The truth of the matter is that they are probably being mean not to. A Yorkie is a small dog and a wire crate, or fancier one, is its haven—it is its and its only!

Traveling in the car, a crate acts for your dog's safety. Should you stop suddenly, your Yorkie will not be thrown forward, or down onto the floor. Your own attention will be on your driving, not watching your dog. If you should have an accident, your Yorkie will not be as likely to be hurt, or be running in terror down a highway if a door is thrown open. You can open the windows in your car without worrying about your Yorkie falling out. The crate provides a cool place for your dog on a hot day as it will be shaded from the sun.

A crate in a motel, hotel, or in a friend's house, protects your Yorkie from being let out of the room should you go out. Often in motels or hotels, small objects like pills, matches or small children's toys get left under beds. Our Yorkie room inspectors have pointed this out to us a number of times, as we have removed these wonderful finds from their mouths. So, if you're not present to protect your pal—crate it!

If traveling by plane, be warned that shipping a dog by air has many risks unless the dog is accompanied. A number of airlines will allow you to travel with your dog in the cabin of the plane if the dog is in a carrier that fits under the seat. Some airlines provide a cardboard carrier for your dog if you do not have one available. If you plan to fly with your dog, you should inquire if the airline of your choice allows it.

Dogs, like people, can get motion sickness while traveling. Most Yorkies are excellent travelers, but if your Yorkie is not one of them, a piece of an antacid tablet will often be the answer. If your veterinarian prescribes other medicine, always try it out ahead of time, while you are still at home. In this way, if your dog should respond adversely to the medicine, you will have your veterinarian at hand. Never give your Yorkie drugs that are not prescribed by a veterinarian, even if they are available in a pet shop.

Well before the turn of the century, his owner's bed has been the Yorkie's favorite sleeping place. *Jeanne Grimsby*

When traveling with your Yorkie, the following packing tips will save worries and perhaps an upset:

1. Its water bowl.
2. Either its own feed dish, or a supply of small paper plates that can be thrown away.
3. Food that your Yorkie is used to eating.
4. A towel of its own.
5. A flashlight for walking your Yorkie at night.
6. A leash.
7. Toys that it's used to.
8. Any necessary medication and a first-aid kit for your Yorkie, containing cures for cuts, stings, itches, diarrhea, and toenail clippers and scissors.
9. A box of tissues or paper towels.
10. A sheet to put on top of the bed, if your Yorkie is a bed-sleeper. (Most of them are!)

Try to stick to feeding and walking your dog at as close to its usual hours as possible. Always take water from home for your dog. If you haven't a lot of room, but are taking a cooler, freeze some water in plastic bottles. It will act as ice for your cooler and, when thawed, you will have more water for your Yorkie. Changing a dog's water from place to place is the best way of being sure your dog will get an upset.

The Yorkshire Terrier—what can you say of him? . . . the most adorable charmer. Ch. Nikko's Rolls Royce Corniche and his daughter, Ch. Nikko's Silver Cloud, owned by Mr. and Mrs. Eddy Nicholson, offer an esthetic indication of why this beautiful breed is so loved by so many.

John L. Ashbey

12

Yorkie Character

In EXTOLLING the virtues of their chosen breed, owners are inclined to wax lyrical about the wonderful things it does, and to proclaim it far superior to any other. Naturally one must assume that they are slightly prejudiced, since they have chosen it above all other breeds to own. Nonetheless, it remains that once a person has owned a Yorkie, there is no doubt he will always own a Yorkie.

The Yorkshire Terrier—what can you say of him? First, he is the most adorable charmer. He always gets his way, even as he pretends to bow to your wishes. He is beautiful in his long, full mantle of blue and gold silk, with neatly placed topknot; but he is fascinating, too, in a straggly, ragged, uneven coat, casting one appealing mischievous eye between scraps of topknot. He is happy being the doll in the doll carriage, acting lookout in a bicycle, lying contendly in the lap of his elderly mistress (or master), watching TV with the boss, or helping to cook dinner with the mistress, one eye cocked to the chance that a tidbit might accidentally fall, which naturally—in order to be a help—it is imperative that he immediately remove from the floor. He's delighted to strut in the show ring and show off in all his glory; or to follow your commands in the Obedience ring, even if—on occasion—he proves his independence by a performance that is his own and not exactly as you'd planned it.

Your Yorkie is happy to share with you—your bed, or anything you eat. He'll gladly accompany you wherever you go or in whatever you do if it can be included.

Be it a big Yorkie or a tiny Yorkie, he is endowed with a marvelous intelligence and a most valiant spirit. He'll teach you he's bigger than any other dog, and that he owns you body and soul—even if you have been under the impression that you owned him. He is, in fact, the perfect companion for all the reasons people keep dogs.

As a watchdog, his hearing is acute and warning will be given as soon as the normal sounds or routine are disturbed. He is not a yappy dog, but will spring to attention should a car be in the driveway, or someone at the door. We've never known anyone who owned a Yorkie in an apartment whose dog could not tell when members of the family were on the ascending elevator.

Yorkies have joined their mistresses and masters in all sorts of jobs. One of the most famous was Pasha—which took on the running of the White House when his Master and Mistress, the Richard Nixons, lived there. One traveled with his master, the captain of a freighter, all through World War II, taking his chances of being torpedoed with his boss while ferrying cargo across the Atlantic. Another has gone to court each day with a court reporter, sleeping in a basket at her feet. One goes to a hospital daily, sitting on her mistress' desk in the administration offices. Fannie Hurst, the author, always had two that slept on her desk while she wrote her novels. Yorkies have supervised gift shops, dress shops, machine shops, dental offices, bookstores, classrooms and interior decorating shops. Many actors and actresses have been accompanied by a Yorkie, both to work and around the world. Two Yorkies were among the hijacked passengers on a plane that was forced to go to Cuba, and the plane was held until Fidel Castro could see the dogs.

The list of travels and jobs that Yorkies have experienced with their bosses could go on and on, but, in truth, it is only an indication of the breed's ability to adapt itself to any situation or circumstance. The tales that follow will, we hope, give those unfamiliar with the breed an idea of what a Yorkie is; those who already know the breed will likely find resemblances to their own Yorkie.

The breed has been used as the canine character in a number of books. The original illustrations done by W. W. Denslow in 1900 for *The Wizard of Oz* were of Toto, the artist's own dog, which was bred by

Helen Hayes's dressing table, by Morgan Dennis.

Illustration of "Pistache" from Albert Payson Terhune's *Real Tales of Real Dogs*, circa 1935.

Mrs. Frederick of Calumet City, Illinois. Hollywood may have used a Cairn for the movie version, but the real Toto was a Yorkshire Terrier.

As to what breed the famous Greyfriars' Bobby was, we'll leave to you to decide, giving only the following quote from *Dogs: Their Points, Peculiarities, Instincts and Whims* edited by Henry Webb, and published in 1872 by Dean and Son, London, England:

> Of the Scotch Terrier (Yorkies were originally called Broken-haired Scotch Terriers) we have still more to add, for Greyfriars' Bobby, the Edinburgh favorite, must not be forgotten, and we cannot do better than to give the following extract from *The Animal World* of May 2nd, 1872: "It is reported that Bobby is a small, rough Scotch Terrier, grizzled (greyish-blue) black with tan feet and nose."

The Yorkie as Hunter

In the early days in Yorkshire, one entertainment enjoyed by Scotchmen and the Yorkshire compatriots was rat-baiting and this tale is given in Robert Leighton's *The Complete Book of the Dog*.

> The local pub was a likely place to see a good sport. As time went on, rats became less easy to obtain and it became fashionable to run handicaps. These were arranged so that the heavier the dog was, the more rats he had to kill. Various handicaps were set ranging from one rat being added to a dog's quota for every three pounds additional weight over his rival, to a rat for every pound. This was, perhaps, the favorite and it was frequent to arrange a handicap where each dog had to kill as many rats as there were pounds in his weight, the dog disposing of his quota the quickest being the winner. This put rather a premium on small dogs and breeds were developed especially for this sport. The smooth black and tan Terriers of Manchester and the rough Yorkshire Terriers were particularly good for this sport, and a friend owns a portrait of three famous Terriers ranging in weight from 5¼ lbs. to 7 lbs.

This type of competition did much to help bring down the size in Yorkie bloodlines.

Mrs. Emma Wilkinson, a well-known English Yorkie breeder, owner of the Gloamin Kennels and a judge of the breed, in writing of the Yorkshire Terrier as a worker, reported: "In 1924, I had a Yorkie bitch bred by my father, Mr. J. Jensess, who was never so happy as when she was going on a ratting spree. Registered as Swanky Girl and weighing about 5 lbs. (and she had three litters), Susan used to be

"First lesson." Trade card for Hood's Sarsaparilla, 1886.

Yorkshire Terriers ratting. Etching by Maud Earl, 1903.

delighted when she was taken down to the farm. When the old steam threshing engine came to thrash corn, Susan used to sit and wait for the chance at a rat, and on one morning she killed 23 rats and was game to go again for more. Susan lived to be 14½ years of age.''

To continue on with their love of hunting, here's a tale told by another famous English breeder, Mrs. Edith Stirk of the Stirkean Kennels, a breeder of many celebrated champions and a well-known judge of the breed:

> I have a first-hand story of one very recent Yorkie's adventures. Her name was Tidy Tiddler and she has just died at the ripe old age of 14 (written in 1967).
>
> I met Tidy at nine weeks when she called to see her Dad, Ch. Stirkean's Chota Sahib, and during the years I was in close touch with her activities. She had six litters all with the greatest of ease, although she was just four lbs., had a coat to the ground, lovely coloring, and was as tough as nails. She took over 14 acres of rabbit infested orchards which were like a wilderness. She bolted 129 rabbits in less than three months. On one occasion she could not be gotten out and they had to dig for her. When she was reached, there were five dead rabbits and Tidy herself was calmly sitting on a tree root ledge. Tidy must have traveled a thousand miles. On one occasion she spotted a rabbit; off she went over field and onto a brook with a covering of thin ice. Down she went but emerged on the other side, shook herself and carried on. Rats were always marked and she would not move until her owner got cracking and got it out.
>
> Her greatest joy was a poacher, the old man of the village. They knew each other like buddies. Tidy could smell him a mile off. She would sit trembling in the window-sill waiting for his approach and the minute she saw him she would hop off her perch, dash out and jump into his pocket and off these two would go for a day's sport. Tidy always brought the dinner home for the other dogs.
>
> Tidy's old friend, the poacher, is now 87 and still tells the story of his great poaching pal.

We have owned many Yorkies whose main joy in life was hunting. Whenever we open our summerhouse, the Yorkies have a field day catching mice, which is greatly appreciated (although it would be nice if they'd refrain from burying them in the slipcovers). Minikin Blue Larkspur, who lived to be fifteen years old, spent most of her summer days either being dragged out of a swamp or lying in the shallow water under the dock catching frogs.

The Yorkie as War Hero

Along with their hunting ability with small game, Yorkies have been war dogs. Though mention has been made of Bill Wynne's Smokey in other books, we feel it must be included here for no record of the breed would be complete without this proud story.

Smokey was a Yorkshire Terrier (seven inches high and four pounds in weight). She was owned by Corporal Bill Wynne of Cleveland, Ohio, and served two years of active duty in the Asiatic and Pacific area during World War II before coming home to live with Bill.

Bill bought Smokey from a buddy who had found her in a foxhole near Nabxab on New Guinea in February 1944. At first it was thought that she belonged to the Japanese, but when she was taken over to the prisoner-of-war camp and an interpreter was gotten to give her commands in Japanese, she didn't understand a word. She didn't understand English either, but her age was estimated to be just a year at that time.

Though she caught cold, shivered and got scared, she lived through 150 air raids on New Guinea, and was a crew member on twelve air-sea rescues without being airsick. Bill Wynne said she was not hard to train and came in very handy on certain types of jobs. Just how handy is best told by him:

> One day while on leave in the town of Lingayen, I was running Smokey through her routine of tricks in a Nipa hut. Bob Capp, of the Communications Section, came up and eyed Smokey suspiciously. He just looked the dog over without saying a word, then finally he said quietly "Bill, we have a long pipe to run a wire through under the airstrip. It is eight inches high and seventy feet long and we are stumped as to how to get the wire through. The wire simply has to go through and we wondered if Smokey could do it. She is small enough and smart too."
>
> We decided to let her have a go at it. Bob brought a ball of string and came along with some linesmen and we all started for the airstrip. The strip had steel matting and when trucks or planes went over it, it was like a thimble on a scrubbing board only amplified a thousand times, which was very nerve racking and ear splitting. We arrived at the bed of the creek in which three culverts, eight inches in diameter, lay side by side. The airstrip ran over the top of them. I knelt and looked through the pipes and saw that soil had sifted through each of the corrugated sections at the joinings, and in some places the pipe was half filled. I picked the one that had the least amount of soil and mold, but

even at that, in some places Smokey would have only four inches of headway. I tied the string to Smokey's collar and made her sit with Bob while I ran to the other end of the culverts. I peeked through the pipe and it seemed totally black except that I could just make out Smokey's outline. The suspense of whether the little dog would do the job was reflected on every face.

She made a few steps and then ran back. "Come Smokey," I said sharply, and she started through again. When about ten feet in, the string caught up and she looked over her shoulder to Bob Capp as much as to say "What's holding us up there?" The string loosened from the snag and she came on again. By now the dust was rising from the shuffle of her paws and as she crawled through the dirt and mold I could no longer see her. I called and pleaded. Not knowing for certain whether she was coming or not. At last, about twenty feet away, I saw two little amber eyes and heard a faint whimpering sound. Those eyes came nearer and at fifteen feet away she broke into a run. We were so happy at Smokey's success that we patted and praised her for a full five minutes.

Smokey ate C-rations, Spam and took vitamin pills. Her bathtub was Corporal Wynne's helmet and her blanket was made from a green felt card table cover.

Smokey owned many decorations, and polled top place in a competition to pick the mascot of the Southwest Pacific Area. In her lifetime, she traveled 40,000 miles giving exhibitions all over the world. At twelve years of age she was still co-starring with her trainer and owner on a weekly TV show over an NBC station in Cleveland, assisting him as he demonstrated how to train your dog. Smokey could spell her name by actually distinguishing the letters and could walk a tightwire blindfolded. Smokey's exploits are a true example of Yorkie courage.

A fact that is not generally known about Smokey is that, in addition to all her other accomplishments, she was a mother. Shortly after Bill acquired her she surprised him by whelping one puppy weighing one ounce at birth. This puppy unfortunately died at six months when disease wiped out some thirty dogs in Bill Wynne's outfit.

Another tale of the Yorkie as a war dog dates from World War I. It concerns a daughter of Eng. Ch. Armley Little Fritz, owned by Tom Hunter, who took her to France with him. This puppy lived in the trenches with Tom Hunter from 1914 to 1918 and from all accounts

Corporal Bill Wynne's "Smokey" in her owner's helmet on the New Guinea battlefield. The helmet doubled as her bathtub.

"Smokey" was able to negotiate a tightrope blindfolded, guided by owner Bill Wynne.

had a great time ratting. Mr. Hunter brought her home safely and she lived to a venerable age of twenty years.

In the Second World War, the French Resistance used many small pet dogs to carry messages as they were very clever and were not as apt to be suspected as were the large dogs normally used for this.

The Navy also had a Yorkie mascot that served on board the U.S.S. *Hassayampa*. This is the tale as told in *The Navy Times*.

> Although most Navy ships have a dog as a mascot, the crew of this tanker is willing to bet that they have the only dog in the fleet with his own special fireplug. (He did have a square yard of sod around his fireplug, but lost it enroute to Hawaii when a heavy sea washed it over the side.) He not only has his own private fireplug, but a personal life jacket and a reserved seat at the movies.
>
> "Boots" is a 4 lb. Yorkie, born in England with a pedigree as long as your arm, and was purchased in London by his owner, the skipper of the ship, Captain M. V. McKraig. He was flown to Philadelphia where he attended the commissioning of the Hassayampa and took up billet as ship's mascot.
>
> Since starting his sea duty, Boots has been thoroughly indoctrinated in the ways of sea-going dogs. He is first at his "abandon ship" station where he waits patiently for one of the men on watch to put his miniature life jacket on for him. He "mans" the quarterdeck when the Captain comes aboard and has never been late for chow call. He is formally listed as "Satan of Gloucestershire" with the English Kennel Club.

The Yorkie as Performer

Yorkies have played parts in many plays, movies, TV shows, the circus and vaudeville acts. As far back as 1908 there are records of their playacting. Pingo appeared in *The Boatman* at Terry's Theater with a St. Bernard that year. Since then they have played many parts.

The appealing looks and beguiling ways of the Yorkie have been featured in advertising campaigns for a wide variety of products. Around 1885 they appeared on premium cards. Premium cards first came into being in 1878 and were in full swing by 1885 with sets of flowers and animals being most popular. Hood's Sarsaparilla used a Scotch Terrier with pups in 1886. Since then they've helped advertise soap, clothing, rugs, stockings, and more recently one appeared in an aspirin commercial on TV. Pogo of Taragon, owned and bred by Swen Swenson, helped Patti Page introduce the song "How Much Is That Doggy in the Window?"

Ella Gast's Yorkie played a part in the memorable *Easter Parade* and several others have had parts in other movies.

Parting Glimpses

Devotees of a breed tend to write excessively of their marvelous attributes. We were prepared to offer here many words of tribute when it was brought to our attention that the breed has the unique ability of being able to speak for itself. Yorkshires like to write autobiographies and, unlike many would-be writers, over the years they have—with the help of fond owners—been capable of having their manuscripts published.

Starting in 1894 when Dick in *Our Dick* wrote of his life in San Francisco, and followed in 1895 when Baba in *The Chronicles of Baba (the Autobiography of Manor House Fly)*, wrote the story of his life, helped by M. Montgomery-Campbell, seven Yorkies—to our knowledge—have gone into print writing of their lives. In 1899, *Loveliness* wrote up her very sad experiences, helped by Elizabeth Stuart Phelps. In 1934, Nick wrote up two years of his life in a book entitled *I'm Nick*, again assisted by an owner—Reginald Callender. In 1938 and 1941 respectively, Tapiola wrote of his adventures in two books: *Journey of Tapiola* and *Tapiola's Brave Regiment*. In 1950 the two books were combined into one, coming out as *The Adventures of Tapiola*. Tapiola's assistant was Robert Nathan. In 1962 Puck wrote his story, helped by Louis Untermeyer, in *The Kitten Who Barked*. And in 1971, Mister got his Mistress, Florence VanWyck, to get his verses about his life published in a book entitled *A Dog's Garden of Verses*. What better source, then, to learn what the Yorkshire is like, than from the mouth and paws of one of these authors?

Nick in *I'm Nick* starts his book with this description:

> I'm a Yorkshire Terrier, so you know what I look like. I'm only a little dog now, just about five pounds is my weight, and so you can imagine what a very tiny person I was when I first remember myself. I was about three months old then, so I must have been a wee little thing when I was born. There must have been almost nothing of me! . . .
>
> I was "Pedigree" you see, and though I hadn't the faintest notion what that meant, I felt it was something important from the awestruck way in which Miss Frenchman said it to people who visited us. At first I was afraid it was a kind of disease, but I found it wasn't. So, as it seemed alright and rather a good thing to have or be—whichever it is—

When it comes to getting along with other animals in a household, size is no problem for a Yorkshire Terrier.

At home, superstars appreciate the company of friends as we all do. Here is Ch. Cede Higgens with his two best friends, Sing Song Charlie and Marlene Lutovsky.

I thought I'd better live up to it. When I got into a fix, I'd say to myself "You're Pedigree" and it helped a lot. You can do a lot if you've got something like that to live up to.

Yorkies have a habit of getting their own way, and can think up tricks to overcome your best plans. One Yorkie always appeared with a woebegone expression, hopping forward on three legs, every time his owners wanted to go out. Having gotten away with it the first time, he would try it every time. Another one was considered too thin, so his owner put down only milk for him to drink. The Yorkie failed to drink the milk and also failed to show any signs of thirst. He was finally caught on top of the grand piano helping himself to water from a large bowl of roses. And when you scold a Yorkie severely, chances are it will end up with you on your knees begging it to please forgive you.

Dr. Gordon Staples in his *Ladies' Dogs as Companions* gives the earliest tale of a Yorkshire Terrier; his sketch of the breed is fun and still true. No Yorkie ever allowed any other breed to be head dog when he was around. The tale is titled "Wagga-Wagga."

My friends often send me hampers. I do not object to this, because they often contain what is very nice, and sometimes what is very curious. Wagga-Wagga came to me in a hamper. Wagga-Wagga is still alive and well, and may be seen any day running about the streets of Twyford, Berks. as independent as a prince.

A short sketch of him may interest and amuse my readers.

When the hamper in question came then, I hastened to undo the fastenings, when, on opening the lid, lo! and behold, Wagga-Wagga.

The first thing that occurred to me was that the doggie was wonderfully small; the second thing that occurred to me was that it was desperately wicked. N.B.—This occurred to me while the animal was holding on to my thumb, very much to his own satisfaction, by his front teeth. Having refreshed himself in this fashion, he condescended to let me put him on the table for further investigation. In size, he is capable of insertion, head foremost, into a pint pot. Color, black, with tan points. Coat, rather long (feather as hard as hairpins), weight, four pounds to a grain. Head, of the cocoanut fashion, and feathered like the body. Eyes, large and round, showing a good bit of the bull, and a large spice of the devil. Of tail, he hasn't a vestige, so there can't be a morsel of controversy on that head. He is pretty straight on his pins, but roaches his back like a cat doing an attitude of defiance. A Collie dog gave him two lines of his mind last week, and he now roaches his back much

A Yorkshire Terrier is ready to do whatever its owner wants. Here, Ch. Rothby's Reneegade, owned by Roberta Rothenbach, appears in a festive mood.

And always remember—no matter how long the coat or elegant the appearance, the Yorkshire is first, last and always a terrier. May it ever remain so.

more. I baptized him Wagga-Wagga on the spot, because he hasn't a tail to wag.

The prevailing disposition of Wagga-Wagga's mind is that of morosity, combined with bad temper. There is nothing on four legs that he won't fly at, and nothing on two either.

This eulogy, written for a Yorkshire Terrier, tells much of the breed's character:

"Quite early in his puppyhood we made the discovery that we were not training him nearly so much as he was training us. He rapidly developed into a kind master, though a very firm one. He was Rooseveltian in his good humor, once his superiority was conceded. After we had learned the meaning of about fifty growls, barks, whines, and gestures, he trained us to perform several tricks under his direction and, when he thought we needed diversion, would engage us in elaborate games. The only time he ever caught a rabbit it turned out to be a skunk, and the only time he caught a bird it was a guinea hen. He hated to be washed, but was inordinately proud of himself when he had been washed and brushed. Taking him for a walk in the city was always an adventure. He became instantly attracted to two kinds of pedestrians—men in dirty clothes and pretty girls in nice clothes—and all other strangers were treated coldly and often with embarrassing rudeness."

Yorkies of today are still convinced they can take on any big dog. The following story appeared in an Associated Press article.

Oliver a twelve pound Yorkie in Buffalo, New York, upon hearing a commotion outside pushed open the screen door of his home to rush out and attack an eighty pound Akita that was attacking an elderly woman. The larger dog broke off the attack when Oliver attacked him. Having diverted the bigger dog, Oliver was smart enough to scamper under a car, while neighbors came to the rescue.

Oliver needed several stitches but he saved the day and showed that the Yorkie of the 1990s is just as intrepid as his ancestors were.

Whether he lives in a palace, a pleasure dome, barn or public house; appears in movies, plays, TV, vaudeville, circuses or exhibitions; is a character in a murder story, love story, an adventure, a child's book or poem; is seen in magazines, newspapers or TV commercials—be it show dog, obedience dog or pet, the Yorkshire Terrier is, above all else, number one companion to its owner.

ISBN 0-87605-361-4

0 21898 00000 2

0 0 3 6 1>
UPC